Remote Cities

Remote Cities

George Franklin

Sheila-Na-Gig Editions

Cover Art: Henri Matisse (French, 1869-1954). *Notre-Dame, une fin d'après-midi* (*A Glimpse of Notre Dame in the Late Afternoon*),1902.
Oil on paper mounted on canvas, support: 28 1/2 x 21 1/2 inches (72.39 x 54.61 cm); framed: 37 x 30 1/4 x 4 inches (93.98 x 76.835 x 10.16 cm). Collection Buffalo AKG Art Museum; Gift of Seymour H. Knox, Jr., 1927 (1927:24). © 2023 Succession H. Matisse / Artists Rights Society (ARS), New York. Photo: Tom Loonan and Brenda Bieger, Buffalo AKG Art Museum.

ISBN: 9798985524277
Library of Congress Number: 2022942513

Sheila-Na-Gig Editions
Russell, KY
Hayley Mitchell Haugen, Editor
www.sheilanagigblog.com

For Ximena—

In the next room, you are writing about your country,
Which is both far away and close to you. From where
I'm sitting, I can hear you whisper.

ACKNOWLEDGMENTS

Many thanks to the editors and staff of the following journals in which these poems have appeared:

Another Chicago Magazine: "Family Letters," "On Tragedy," "The Ship of Theseus"

Black Coffee Review: "Pat Down by the X-Ray Machine," "What Dying Is Like"

Cagibi: "Two Years Later"

Consequence: "Achilles' Valet"

Degenerate Art Journal: "Apollo and Marsyas"

First Literary Review—East: "Beyond the Pleasure Principle"

KAIROS Literary Magazine: "Cold Tea," "From a Distance"

KGB Bar Lit: "July," "The Day I Invented God"

MacQueen's Quinterly: "Alcestis," "Funeral Rites," "Orphic Mysteries"

Matter: "For a Friend Who Looks Out Hospital Windows"

Meat for Tea: The Valley Review: "A Brief Introduction"

Nagari: "Another October Night"

New York Quarterly: "The Ghost of Juan Ramón Jiménez Has Coffee at Starbucks"

Ocotillo Review: "The End of the Republic"

One: "Sir Bedivere in Iowa"

Panoply: "Heisenberg in the Suburbs," "In the Absence of Coffee," "I Wish I Understood Love"

Red Ogre Review: "Ghosts," "Poem Written to Win a Contest," "Real Monsters"

Revista Abril: "Reading Orwell in Colombia"

Sequestrum: "Muscovy Ducks," "'Such was the funeral of Hector, breaker of horses,'" "The Ape in the Garden," "Visitors"

Sheila-Na-Gig online: "A Dalliance of Crows," "A Lesson," "Afternoon in November," "At the Art Institute of Chicago," "A Walk at Dusk," "Bellini's *Annunciation*," "Black Olives," "Eclipse," "Incense and Straw," "In the Bad Old Days," "In the Last Days of an Empire," "Odysseus," "On a Blue Tarp," "Palm Fronds," "Preparations," "Remote Cities," "Stewed

Fruit," "Sunday," "Written on Papyrus," "Writing about Your
  Country"
South Florida Poetry Journal: "At the Next Table," "Pastiche"
TAB: The Journal of Poetry & Poetics: "Crows"
Tar River Poetry: "Staying Up Late"
The Comstock Review: "Museum," "Upper West Side"
The Curator: "Of Arms and the Man"
The Ekphrastic Review: "Cuernavaca"
The Inflectionist Review: "Illegible"
The Lake: "Angelus Novus"
The MacGuffin: "In Oak and Hickory"
The Woven Tale Press: "In a Suburb," "Lunch in Hartford," "Science
  Fiction in Canton Palace," "Sonnet"
Thimble: "Teaching Walt Whitman in a Prison in Florida"
Twyckenham Notes: "On the Dogana's Steps"
Willows Wept Review: "Pastoral of the Alligator Farm"

Contents

IV.

The night stays chilly, the stars brighter.

V.

I invented God in the late afternoon in October.

VI.

The rapid clicks that sounded like rain.

VII.

I wasn't dying. Your white shoulders proved it.

VIII

We don't know who is safe and who isn't.

IX.

From where I'm sitting, I can hear you whisper.

I.

I touch your nightgown folded beneath the pillow.

Sunday

In the future that doesn't exist yet, I
Wake sluggishly on a Sunday, press
Dry lips against your shoulders and neck,
Wrap my leg over yours and, still half dreaming,
Let my hand drift across your breasts, down
To the sheets twisted by gyrations
Of love and sleep. Morning light
Evades the shutters, reveals the wall
By the closet, the Chinese calligraphy
Framed above the desk—the one a monk gave me
Forty years ago—and the chair where your robe
Waits, folded, patient, nearly as smooth
As your skin beneath my hand.
In the future that doesn't exist yet, we
Will eventually be missing. I don't remember
What the calligraphy means. I think it has
Something to do with emptiness and form,
How even when we're here, like this,
It's not for long. But we don't need
Calligraphy to tell us that. We hold each other
For a while and then make coffee.

SONNET

There's something absolute about the past.
The Trojan war and last night's birthday dinner
Are equally out of touch. We fool ourselves
That memory makes one close at hand, the other
Dust and recited story. Candles blown out
Have *disappeared*. That word is like a zero,
Absence, the view from the astronaut's visor
Surrounded by black (*what?*) between the stars.
We cover up our loss with words for nothing,
And grammar gives us what facts can't. Memory's
Unreal, an epic with a vague beginning,
No ending to speak of, lives written badly.
I know all this, but it doesn't make a difference.
I touch your nightgown folded beneath the pillow.

FLAMINGOS AND MONKEYS

We got word yesterday about the house near Rio Cali.
There are excavators digging up the foundations, the steps
That went up the hill, the basement with the terrazzo floor

Where you would go to study. You took me there once,
And a security guard let us in to look around. It was supposed

To be a real estate office, selling homes that looked out
On stunning green landscapes somewhere in Valle del Cauca.
It wasn't clear where. Actually, there was a lot that wasn't clear.

No one was in the office, just a bunch of empty workstations—
Everything was spotless. We looked at each other and

Nodded. Money laundering doesn't require much in the way
Of employees, but the guard was bored and nice to us, opening
The door so we could go downstairs. I saw the boulder in

The side yard where you used to sit, and I imagined your family
Eating dinner inside, your father getting the largest portion,

Then you, the oldest sister. Next door, there was a church and
Up the hill, Zoológico de Cali, full of flamingos and monkeys
Calling across the walkways in late afternoon, when the sun dropped

Behind the mountains. This weekend, we're staying in your
Apartment in Miami, going for walks along the bay, looking

At the old houses surrounded by new construction. How long
Before the excavators arrive here as well, the houses pulverized,
Carted away to become landfill? From the tenth floor of your building,

We watch the sun sink behind warehouses and railroad tracks,
Final rays lighting up the red anthuriums and orchids in your

Living room, the piles of books on your bedroom table. Here,
The flamingos are mostly on postcards, and no monkeys
Call to each other across darkening avenues or parking lots.

I go into the kitchen and open the bottle we bought of *vino tinto*.
Soon, it will be time to make dinner.

CROWS

It's not dawn yet, but a few birds are
Already awake—no stars, just clouds
Drifting east across a darker sky.
I didn't plan to get up early.
The words, *lo siento*, repeated
In my sleep. Was I the one speaking?
Siento mucho tu pérdida.
The sky has opened just enough for
The trees to turn black, and the birds
Become more persistent. There are so
Many losses these days. I could have
Been dreaming about any of them.
Siento mucho tu pérdida.
In a few minutes, the sky lightens.
I think I can make out crows flying
Above the high fronds of a palm tree,
Wing-shapes outlined by fading clouds, but
At this dim hour, all birds are crows.

Two Years Later

Two years ago, we flew to Colombia. Your father
Had died in Cali, and you'd asked that the funeral

Be delayed until we arrived. His body waited for us,
Dressed in neatly pressed clothes, in bronze make-up

To give his cheeks color. Your nephew put a drawing
In the casket, and everything went smoothly

Like the conveyor belt that took your father behind
A curtain and on to cremation, there or somewhere else—

I wasn't sure. We stayed in San Antonio, far away
From your family and your friends, whitewashed buildings,

Narrow sidewalks, and terracotta tiles, a steep hill
Leading up to a church—at night, motorcycles

And people dancing, cafés with the hiss of
Espresso machines, couples standing in doorways,

Talking in low voices. We stayed in San Antonio,
And we walked on the narrow sidewalks and smelled

The coffee and rolls coming from the bakery, the
Only place open on Sunday morning. Two years

Isn't that long, but long enough for everything to change,
For the world to have stopped, to have buried its dead,

Restarted, stopped again, and buried more. All the while,
In a neighborhood in Miami of wooden townhouses, half-empty

Malls, and apartment buildings that are showing their age,
We've done what they call "sheltering in place," waiting

For the sickness to be over, the equilibrium to return.
We still hold each other at night, lips touching lips,

Hands tracing the contours of our bodies, reminding
Each other that we're still alive, still full of memories

Of walking down narrow sidewalks, of whitewashed
Buildings, of music spilling out of clubs and restaurants,

Of rough sheets that still smell of the laundry, of desire
Stronger than grief.

—March 12, 2021

STAYING UP LATE

The dog comes in from outside, trailing
Oak leaves and mud, worn out from chasing
The big opossum who lives under

The wooden deck in the backyard. He
Sinks down next to my desk, satisfied
That the marsupial invasion's

Been thwarted, at least for the moment.
If you were here, you'd sniff, shake your head,
And laughing exclaim, "*¡Huele feo!*"

But, it's Tuesday night, and you're downtown
At your apartment, writing, and I'm
Supposed to be writing too. Instead,

I watch bad science fiction and stay up
Because I'm too tired to go to sleep.
(I know that doesn't make any sense,

But that's what happens when you're not here.)
On Thursday, when you return, I'll bake
That fresh rosemary bread you like,

Sauté a *tortilla* with onions,
Potatoes, and mushrooms that I've fried
Till they're just turning brown, and open

A bottle of the good cabernet
We've saved. Then we'll have *cafecitos*,
Translate poems or read for a while,

And agree with great solemnity
That this time we really will get to
Bed at a reasonable hour.

I Wish I Understood Love

You open the outdoor shutters so the room won't seem so
Dim and small—papers, books in piles on the bed tables, the desk,
My old shirts and pants crowding the closet with its broken door,

The one I promised to fix at least two years ago. You work
Through the afternoon, translating while you listen to Rimsky-Korsakov,
Your back to the window, your hands casting shadows, puppets,

Their strings falling, rising, with the music. After dinner, we have coffee
And go for a night walk by the shopping mall. Only a few restaurants
Are still open—and the new 7/11 with neon gas pumps. Clouds

Seem to stumble across the dark sky to the west.
Beneath the streetlamps, there are pink mussaenda blossoms,
Orange-red poinciana framed by black, and those

Yellow allamanda vines we can barely see on top of the fence.
Across the street, the supermarket is just closing. I know how
Fragile all this is, how lucky I am to walk next to you here,

Talking about grammar, Octavio Paz, Borges,
Or the *pan de bono* you used to buy at a bakery in Cali—
You tell me it's not there anymore, but there must be others that

Are just as good. Tomorrow, we will sleep past the alarm, having
Gone to bed late, having stayed up, wasting time, trying to find
A poem I wanted to show you, sending email to friends we don't see

Very often. Finally, we will have turned back the bed, slipped our legs
Simultaneously under the blanket, arranged the pillows and set
The alarm we'll sleep past, then touched, lips pressed fiercely

Against whatever parts of each other we can find. I wish
I understood love. I call you, *mi amor*, but in Miami, the ladies who
Pour *cortaditos* at every *cafeteria* use that expression all the time.

I worry the words don't mean enough, but I don't know what
Words would mean more. For dinner, you fried fish Colombian-style,
Pescado aborrajado, while I made rice and cut cherry

Tomatoes to put over the avocados. We drank red wine and talked.
Afterwards, cleaning up, I tried out some sentences in my very
Bad Spanish to make you laugh, succeeding beyond all expectations.

The Ghost of Juan Ramón Jiménez Has Coffee at Starbucks

He's spent all morning walking in Coral Gables,
Remembering canals and looping streets as they'd looked
When he lived here, sorrow hanging from the banyan trees,
Their thin, brown roots reaching for earth, Campo Sano,
The hospital where he'd been treated for depression, smells
Of disinfectant, his house near the campus, the large
Green lawns and barrel-tiled roofs of middle-class mansions,
Imitations of an imaginary Spain, noise of South Dixie Highway
Inescapable, even at an inside table. At the university library,
He'd opened the encyclopedia and smiled that Franco was dead—
No need to be ashamed of that smile. He'd smiled also at
The women crowding the counter, placing orders for sweet drinks.
Even dead, he missed Zenobia and wondered what she would
Say if she could see him, drinking bad coffee, examining
SUVs and bicycles in the parking lot—he looks up suddenly to see
A blue and gold macaw perched on a high branch, the world
Still capable of surprise.

A Dalliance of Crows

I'd never heard a crow sing before—cawing, yes, plenty of that—
Until you called me over to the big window that looks out on
    the garbage cans.
Two crows were perched there, large, black, glossy feathers,
    shadows on the window shade.
The sound was embarrassingly pure. No dove or thrush ever
    did better.
I read later this was their courtship ritual, an intimate moment
We probably shouldn't have observed. We didn't mean to
    be voyeurs,
But there we were, listening until they flew away.

ANOTHER OCTOBER NIGHT

They say in Japan it's a terrible thing
To be a hungry ghost, drifting unsatisfied
Through the lives you've left behind,

Calling out forever for some part of you
That's always missing. The wind
From the east brings rain, clouds moving

Quickly across the night sky, palm fronds
Stretched straight, then dropped, the powerlines
By the canal rocking and creaking slightly.

Perhaps, on one of those nights I'll be there
In the corner of your eye, an animal,
Unidentifiable in the dark, crossing the street,

Climbing down from a wall. I wouldn't want
To frighten you, so I might stay distant,
In the shadow of an allamanda vine

Or the headlights of a passing car—just
A glimpse and then gone. Or, if I'm lucky,
I'll find myself in the soft air

Touching your face as you walk that
Narrow asphalt path by the canal, a breeze
Smelling of salt, of the roots of plants that grow

In damp soil, and you'll stop and look up
And recognize my voice in the rumble of traffic
Or in the wind swaying the powerlines.

Of course, there're no hungry ghosts,
In Japan or here, and all that's left of me
Will be ashes kept in a cardboard box or a small urn

With the label of a funeral home glued underneath—
But that part's not important. If, on some
October night, you remember our walks or something

I said that made you laugh, it'll be enough.

II.

The boat filled with samurai never moves.

On Tragedy

Loneliness is the very essence of tragedy....
        —Georg Lukács

Lukács says we want to feel at home in the world, or at least, want
    our loneliness to count for something. Instead, we wipe grief off
    our shoes every time we come inside, but an odor lingers, the
    hamper of clothes that should have been washed, the moldy
    scent from behind the refrigerator.
When the dog comes in, he brings with him a smell of rotting leaves.
Was there ever a before to this after?
When you walk at night in the rain, there are smears of color on black
    asphalt, stoplights and blinking signs, low clouds turned a dark
    orange by reflection, restaurants that have closed early.
Was it ever different? I will tell you a story.

It will be a story about a king because the problems of kings are
    different from my problems or yours. The king's dinner is
    always prepared by others and served by well-dressed footmen
    and polite maids.
Kings never wash their own dishes or clean under the bed or behind
    the couch. Their concerns are invasions and crop failures, the
    curses of sorcerers, betrayals by greedy cousins.
In the midst of such things, most care little for philosophy. Unlike
    the poets and scholars, they are at home wherever they wander.
    Peasants, shopkeepers, even bankers, take off their hats and bow.
    A child with long curls rushes up with flowers,
Which the king will pass to an assistant with an indulgent smile.

In this story, the king thought nothing was wrong until the gods,
    who are believed to have created us for their entertainment, sent
    a horrible plague, a fever that killed whole families and caused
    the king's city to come to a stop. For the first time, the king did
    not feel at home.

A rumor surfaced, a kind of reasoning: if there is something wrong
in the city, there must be something wrong with the king of the
city, for the king's body is the body of the city.

The priests could offer no help. Do they ever, in any story? But an
old prophet put it directly, told the king: "It's your fault."

For those of you who don't already know this story, the king had
killed his father without knowing that was his father and then
married his mother without knowing she was his mother, so he
had children who were also his brothers and sisters,

And finally he recognized there was absolutely nothing he knew
about anything.

The king who was no longer a king spent the rest of his life homeless
and blind as a red earthworm beneath the soil.

Tonight, when it's raining and even the dog doesn't want to go
outside, I think of that king who had felt perfectly at home for so
long. I think of his sister-daughters who travelled with him,
whose names no one wanted to speak.

I like to believe that on a night like this they would have found
shelter and a bowl of soup, wine to ward off the bone chill, the
smell of wet wool, smell of pig shit and oxen shit, the sour straw
beneath their heads.

And the king who was no longer a king? I imagine him staying up
most of the night, which to him was now the same as day. He
would have listened to the grunts and snorts of the animals, to
their sudden belches, their unembarrassed farts.

He would have been listening until he too fell asleep,

Trying to understand what language it was they were speaking.

In the Bad Old Days

In the bad old days, Russian poets
Memorized each other's manuscripts
So there'd be nothing to confiscate
Or burn. In Truffaut's film, *Fahrenheit
451*, the camera, more
Elegant than Bradbury's prose, tracks
His Book People crisscrossing on
Forest paths, reciting to themselves,
Repeating the books they'd become and
Would pass on. I regret I know so
Few poems by heart—some Donne and Blake,
Browning, Edward Lear, Auden and Frost—
Mostly poems Brodsky required us
To write from memory, sitting around
That cluttered seminar table in
An overheated room. I recall
Shivering on the Amtrak platform
In a wet wind, drilling "Afterwards"
Into my brain, one line at a time,
Listening to Hardy speculate
About his own death, stepping back to
Let the express train go by. Poems
Give shape to memory, then become
Memories themselves, preserved in gray
Tissue, neurons joining synapses,
Express trains headed north along the
Hudson River, Hardy's pattern of
Anapests and iambs repeated
On my dull American tongue—the
Camera pans to Julie Christie
And Oskar Werner as they, without
Realizing, pass each other in
The woods, remembering, reciting.

INCENSE AND STRAW

Tonight, my leg hurts, and my eyes are tired.
I read Mandelstam's poem for Tsvetaeva,
Moscow in 1916, the sled they'd hired
Careening through dirty snow, chapel of a

Church with an onion dome, not a white-spired
Arrow that penetrates heaven, or Platonic love,
Poisonously insipid, weakly desired,
Not Protestant either, but lit by candles above,

Below the altar; outside, smell of horse merde,
The beast exhaling steam, its crusted hooves
Knocking against the ice, the driver's black beard

Rocking along as he snores; inside, a dove's
Dry feather against her cheek, prayers unheard—
The moon like ripe garlic breaks into cloves.

At the Art Institute of Chicago

There's a crowd gathered to see Edward
Hopper's *Nighthawks*—Ximena and I
Are still cold from the chill outside. It's
November, and we've just checked our coats.
From the back of the room, we see the
Other visitors more closely than
We see details in Hopper's painting,
A tall couple, from Europe maybe,
Dressed in matching black leather jackets,
Colorful sneakers, the backs of their
Heads moving at different angles,
A group of women, old friends I think,
Midwestern, in their fifties, blue jeans
And wool sweaters. Some kids are standing
Up close to the canvas, in college
Or art school. Everybody's eyes are
Looking at the light shining from the
Diner's yellow walls and white ceiling.
That's when I notice we're all standing
In front of the counter, pulled in by
What we recognize: three faces that
Are exposed, and one turned away, the
Metal urns of coffee, the narrow
Door, the empty stools for customers
Who aren't there. No one stands in front of
The larger part of the painting, dark,
Nothing human about it, a store
That's probably out of business, a
Deserted building, street without cars.
It's like an old magician's trick from
A carnival—misdirection. We
All look at the faces, thinking there's
A backstory we can understand.
The woman with the red hair and red
Dress was Hopper's wife. The man smoking
A cigarette has a beak-shaped nose.

I edge left and stand by the greens and
Blacks of the street, the soot-smooth brick of
The tenement, dirty windows where
No one's drawn the shades, where there's no sign
Anyone's ever lived there. Why do
Those faces keep staring over that
Counter? Why don't the customers get
Up and leave? The woman dressed in red
Holds something in her hand and never
Takes her eyes off it. Is it money?
Don't let the woman's hand distract you.
Keep looking at the doorways, the street.

Angelus Novus

They were stopped on the Spanish side of the border,
Having crossed the mountains into Catalonia.
There were orders to return all refugees back to Vichy.
The police would be waiting, internment, then Germany,
If he wasn't shot first. That night he stared at the bottle
Of morphine on the bedtable, made certain his manuscript
Was in the suitcase, folded his shirts, and put his shoes
Outside the door, as though he were leaving them
To be cleaned and polished. He would have liked
To have listened to music again, to read a few more
Books and write some letters. There was always so much
More to say, to find out in the saying. Hannah had
The essay on history. She'd get it out, to England or
America. He looked again at his visa permitting him
Entry to the promised land, the Statue of Liberty, survival.
Now, it was just a scrap of paper and meant nothing.
He remembered Klee's painting of the *Angelus Novus*,
How the angel moved backwards into the future, eyes
Fixed on the utter wreck of the past. You don't look at
A painting like that, he thought. It looks at you.
Soon, it would be time to turn off the light.

BLUE AND WHITE TILES

The tiles reflect the streetlamps, the glare
Of moonlight that reaches us from far
Away. The lips of conversos no
Longer mumble prayers. No candles
Are lit on the sabbath, hidden by
The tiles and high wooden door. Only
The noise of car tires taking a curve
And voices of passersby drift through
The cold air of the mountains. A few
Blocks away, the books in the Bishop's
Library sleep undisturbed by mice,
Doctrine, or politics. The man who
Owned the house covered in stars must have
Known the Inquisition would someday
Throw open his door, seize everything,
But the gesture was worth it: each day,
Inquisitors would have stared at the
Tiles unable to act. Even when
They took him to Mexico City
To burn, the blue and white tiles remained.

Octavio Paz

I knew almost nothing about his life in India.
I imagined saris and white shirts, carvings of
Shiva and Parvati, diplomatic receptions,
Meetings certainly, but no one would have
Cared much about Mexico's position on
Kashmir or East Pakistan. In class, though, I asked
Him about the title "Ladera Este," whether it
Had anything to do with Su Tung-Po. His face
Lifted. In manuscript, there'd been an epigraph,
Later cut, and in English, his publisher thought
"Eastern Slope" sounded like a ski resort. He said
India was a kind of exile, the way Su Tung-Po might
Have felt in his cottage, far away from power,
Emperor and court carrying on without him,
Without his poems or advice. Outside, green mangos
Ripened, hanging from branches. Monkeys
Woke up suddenly, calling to each other at night,
Cries, threats, snarls. He didn't talk about the dirty
War, the massacre in 1968, or his resignation, anger,
Return to Mexico. Instead, he remembered a
Conversation with Breton about automatic writing,
His poem about De Sade—which wasn't automatic at all,
But Breton still liked it—and going to parties with
Roman Jakobson. Then he looked at us, notebooks
Open, leaning forward in our chairs, and remarked,
"It's so odd, attending a university to study poetry."

CUERNAVACA

For Omar Villasana

In the cathedral at Cuernavaca, fish
Wait below the blue surface, teeth bared.
A ship filled with samurai cruises above them,
Each armed with machete or halberd—
Conquistador samurai—while captured missionaries
Follow in another boat.

          Beyond the wooden
Doors, afternoon turns the courtyard white.
Vendors sell flowers, hats, toys,
And across the narrow street, that's us talking
In the shade, drinking cold beer,
Waiting for evening.

          Emperor Maximilian
Bought a place here for his mistress. *Bought*
May be too polite a word for it. The house was,
As they say, a forced sale. It came complete with
Gardens, cool in summer, mild in winter.
They didn't enjoy it for long.

          In the cathedral at
Cuernavaca, on the stone above the heavy
Wooden door, fish with sharp teeth
Wait below the blue surface
Of the sea. The boat filled with samurai
          Never moves.

THE SHIP OF THESEUS

On the windowsill in winter, a plastic jug half full of cider
Turning hard overnight, a wind that blows out feelings,
Candleflame gone dark, gone nowhere.

I went to college in an old hotel, wool carpet lining
The hallways, a fire-escape leading to the roof, a view
Of the mountains. The hotel was white, and the mountains

Were white. Yellow snowplows snailed their way
Toward Bethlehem and Littleton. We played chess
And talked about the Iliad, sat on the steps, drank brandy.

On the other side of the earth, the Vietnam War
Dragged on (Saigon hadn't fallen yet), and Nixon
Was still president. You could hear the wind piling up

High drifts of snow, covering cars in the parking lot.
I was living that year with a girlfriend on the fourth floor,
A room that faced sunrises, pine, and maple. The neighbors

Could hear us making love in the morning while
It was still dark, a red handkerchief thrown over the lamp.
The radio station was in the basement and played

Billie Holiday or whatever the students who were up late
Requested. My friend, Tom, from back then, died last year,
And I've lost track of most of the others. Once, a card

Arrived from the girlfriend, apologizing but not
Saying why. On the envelope, she was careful not to write
A return address. I feel pretty much the same way.

Whoever we all were in 1973, we're not anymore. Only
Our names are the same, for the most part, and a few
Embarrassing memories. We're like that Ship of Theseus

Plutarch describes in Athens, each plank having rotted
And been replaced, the philosophers equally divided
Whether it was still the same ship.

Upper West Side

Central Park a month ago, we walked south skirting the Reservoir,
the sun starting to sink behind pre-war buildings and into the
Pacific, thousands of miles away.

At 86th Street, we cut over to walk past the restored brownstones,
then west on 85th where I used to live opposite the high school.
It was a tougher neighborhood then: bottles thrown from rooftops,
burglaries, even shooting.

One night, I saw a man in an overcoat breaking into parked cars with
a crowbar. He held it up and looked at me, as though he expected
me to try to talk him out of it. I didn't.

There was a bar at the corner that's not there anymore. It wasn't a
place I frequented, but I would give it a quick glance when I
walked my chow before bed.

He was a black mountain of fur with a purple tongue and a bad
disposition. People tended to leave us alone, and our
apartment wasn't one that got burgled.

Still, he and I jumped behind a car when two or three guys tumbled
out of that bar's door and, as they say, shots were fired.

Now, it's all clothing shops and restaurants with regional specialties
from Italy or somewhere in Spain.

It was Sunday, and they were cleaning up after brunch. Nobody was
shooting at anybody else. It was just getting colder as the shadows
of buildings fell across Amsterdam Avenue and Broadway.

We walked north, back to Patricia's. At least, I didn't pretend to feel
nostalgic. Forty-some-aught years ago, I'd lived in a dark New
York apartment. There'd been a window opening on trees, but
I remember it as dark.

My marriage felt like a play written by Strindberg but discarded as
too loveless and angry to be real.

My late-night walks with the dog were escapes from arguments begun
at dinner, trips to the cash machine to check the balance, which
was never good. Sometimes, we had loud fights on the street,
which were worse.

Walking up Amsterdam that day, I tried to tell you about some of
this, but looking at that white-brick apartment building on a
quiet block, a good neighborhood,
There's no sign it ever happened.

III.

Give them that Greek coin in your pocket.

"Of Arms and the Man"

Aeneas leans his hand against a palm tree,
Rough to the touch and real—his gods appear
As dreams, as voices, mists, hallucinations.
Walking by Dido's palace, Aeneas stops,
Listens for flutes and drums, a song he knows,
Carried and dropped—the sky lit up with flares
And antiaircraft weapons. Sandstone scrapes
Across his fingers. Burnt fields are ploughed with salt.
In Rome, boxes of dates from Libya,
Sicilian blood oranges, olive oil
In shades of green to gold—clusters of grapes
Circled by flies with iridescent wings—
Scipio's legionnaires are followed by vultures.
The past circles the future, silver drones
Hover like clouds over Ilium's bricks, Anchises
A sack of grain on Aeneas's shoulders, Creusa,
Who couldn't keep up, lost in the smoke and shadows,
Dido, her hair scented with jasmine blossoms,
Lost in the smoke and shadows, the date palms
Heavy with fruit, wind carrying the scent
Of jasmine, ash, salt, and automobile
Exhaust—a woman's face that turns away.

In a Suburb

In a suburb of Austin, Texas,
A butterfly dreams he's a Chinese
Philosopher. All the garage doors

On the block open their mouths to take
Communion. You say it's sad when stars
Collapse into themselves. I agree,

But when Zarathustra met himself
In the garden, the earth did not stop
Turning, though the prophets who'd entered

Had all gone mad. Who is that sitting
On the stone bench, up ahead in the
Shadows? Rabbi Akiba

Entered in peace and left in peace. Still,
I think there is something wrong with the
World. In that dream, Nestor appeared. He

Wanted to speak, but the sounds from his
Tongue were not the speech of the Nestor
We knew, but guttural then shrieking,

The language of apes or men dying.
The war had been a war of desire.
All the men wanted Helen, and black

Carrion birds ate the genitals
And eyes of heroes. In the cornfield
At Antietam, bullets closer than

Corn stalks, the dead prone, in formation.
Which of us was deceived more, you who
Woke to your clothing and mirror, to

The same face yawning, the same voice rough
With sleep, or me awake even in
Sleep, my wings covered in dust, floating?

REMOTE CITIES

Built on the edge of lakes and rivers,
Remote cities, brown wooden buildings,
Narrow underground passages that

Crawl one cellar to another but
Never emerge beneath the white sky.
Their labyrinths have no Theseus,

And you have no ball of thread or sword.
The monster that was waiting for you
Gave up a long time ago. He's gone

To a cave in the mountains, washes
Down whole sheep with rainwater, picks his
Teeth with something you don't want to see.

You'll never get the chance to say your
Name is No Man, to hear prophecies,
Negotiate with gods and witches.

The wind changed direction, and somehow
You missed each other. There's a sign that
Reads, "The stationmaster will be back

After lunch." Someone is giving birth
Behind the sofa. Cracked bones are strewn
Across a beach, cigarette filters

With lipstick, turtle shells carved into
Ashtrays, smells of rotting fish, seaweed.
On a cold train platform, a shopping

Bag spills open, dust burns your eyelids,
And someone you almost recognize
Falls onto the tracks—a saxophone

Plays ballads no one can hear but you.
Give thanks to the veiled inhabitants
Of these cities, generous with their

Salt and black bread, their bowls of water
That reflect your face. Let them draw close.
Give them that Greek coin in your pocket.

"Go tell the Lacedaemonians"

Go tell the Lacedaemonians that Persian rule
Wouldn't have been so bad, that taxes are a necessary evil,
And the Great King only requires obedience.

Go tell the Athenians that the flight of birds, even owls,
Is meaningless, tell them not to be deceived by clever speakers,
By sophists who believe all questions have answers.

Go tell the Sibyl that the god's breath was hot with falsehoods,
And that the words she spoke but does not remember
Were random as dreams and less substantial than ash or smoke.

Stranger, when you get to Lacedaemon, passing souvenir shops
And satellite dishes, hotels and petrol stations, pensioners
Arguing in the street, ask them for us once more

Why we lie here, having followed their orders.

The End of the Republic

When exactly did it end? Perhaps a general
Crossed a river or troops were used to quell
A riot, perhaps the senate simply failed
To meet one day, the lawmakers deciding
To sleep in, get a massage after breakfast,
Perhaps a tribe from Central Asia invaded
India or a young noble somewhere announced
He was a god—I spent all afternoon in
The library, opening scrolls to find the answer,
But the histories of that period were unavailable.
They said the Emperor himself had requested them,
And it might be many years before they were
Returned. I thought to check the accounts written
In other languages, Greek, Hebrew, dialects
Of eastern tribes. None of them could give me
More than hints. An old librarian implied
He might be able to answer my questions if we got
To know each other better after work,
But I declined. He had a large pustule on
His left cheek, and his breath smelled of purgatives.
When I returned home, my mother asked me what
I'd been studying, and I explained. She gave me
One of her looks that suggests some combination
Of pity and amusement. "The republic," she said,
"Was ended before it began. Citizens desire
To be entertained more than bothered with governing."
I didn't argue with her. My mother's opinions
Are more fixed than constellations, which at least
Cross the sky each night. Tomorrow, I'll return
To the library. There must be scrolls no one has read.

Saturn Devoured by His Children

Leopardi wrote a dialogue between fashion and death,
Both revolving in the danse macabre of a medieval clock,
The progress of clouds filmed and speeded up, rushing

Outside the frame where we no longer see them or
Seeming to materialize from nothing. Pound said to
"Make it new," but I'm not so sure of that anymore.

Maybe I've reached an age where novelty, fashion, and death
Are too much alike. I tell *mi compañera* that I'm
Un viejo cascarrabias. No te metas conmigo. I'm only

Half joking. A poem should feel smooth in your hand,
Words to come with stories attached, a sheaf of music
Hidden in the lining of an old jacket, smuggled by

Customs where you give the officer a smile and say
How happy you are to be home. He'll stamp
Your papers with the date and port of entrance

And even wave as you walk through the doors and
Down the shiny hallway. Cerberus, who sniffs
Out history, will move on to other suitcases, other

Travelers. For all he knows, you're as modern
As a cellphone that reads thoughts or the fountain
Of youth in a squeeze-tube. He, like other monsters of the new,

Will let you pass unharmed, unaware you are a spy
Dispatched by the ancients to remind of epigraphs carved
By alien visitors and prophecies whispered by wood nymphs.

Nietzsche and Borges were right. Everything returns, including
The new, where Saturn is devoured by his children.
Fedoras reappear. Narrow neckties again grow wide.

Poor, unhappy Leopardi, his unhappiness unhappily to be repeated,
And Pound to return to the madhouse, sneaking
Anti-Semitic winks to his fascist visitors. Eliot thought

The meaning of tradition was altered by each new addition—
The new become the past changed by the future or an old man
Become a child, sadder even than Leopardi.

In Defense of Esotericism

It's all right not to be understood. The gray
Sponge in the skull absorbs both blood and gravy.

What's old, they tell us, is only here because
The powerful found it useful, their image

Mirrored in this painting, that play. Other stuff
Was just as good. But antique or obscure has

Its own appeal, not wholly deliberate,
Flickering mind-lit figures, blue silhouettes

Of willow trees in Spode porcelain, China stone
And kaolin, bone ash from slaughterhouses,

Philosophies first conceived in sour taverns
Where customers shoved dirty arms and spoons deep

In a pot for scraps of half-boiled meat, and ale
Or cider aged with a rat in the barrel,

If it aged at all. Still, language, you respond,
Is mind itself. Revolution begins with

Shaping thought, with stories of child wizards and
Villains not too elegant in their speech. Let

Them eat websites and cable news and grind their
Teeth at night dreaming of conspiracy while

Green lizards navigate a burnt cathedral.
Let Rilke keep his angels, Pound his fascist

Conjuring. The future already happened
And seems ready to happen again. Why should

A poem sell itself to you so cheaply?

The Ape in the Garden

Mahler complained to Freud how the vulgar
Intrudes on the sublime, the organ grinder's jangle
On choking grief, the ape in the garden, wild
Gesticulations in moonlight. He imagined
Alma in bed with Gropius, convulsions of
Her abdomen and pelvis, and worst of all,
That he was old and no longer mattered.
Even Earth is not immortal. That first morning
In Dublin, I heard horses' hooves in the street.
Outside, a wagon delivering milk. The landlady's
Husband read Yeats to his children. America
Was somewhere far away, a landscape painting
Of wilderness and sunlight, the occasional
Indigenous settlement, no hint of political violence.
Garfield was shot by a campaign worker in dirty clothes,
Who'd wanted a job in Paris. In Vienna, there
Were swastikas chalked on the sidewalk outside
House No. 19, Berggasse. Memory of the ratcatcher's
Window, of stuffed rodents, feral cats. *The sky is*
Always blue, the Earth secure. Forever, forever.
In London, "the familiar siren-shrieks, the alerts,"
"The all-clear." Freud to HD: "The trouble is—
I am an old man—*you do not think it worth*
Your while to love me."

The Toilet of Venus

The weathered bench in the backyard is not
The throne of a goddess, just a bench where
No one sits anymore. Damp with rain, circled
By mosquitoes, it presides over nothing except
The green spots of algae that grow on its back,
Armrests, and seat. *Poikilothron*, Sappho
Called the place where Aphrodite rested: dappled,

Ornate, even spotted like a leopard skin or
Embroidered with flowers—no one knows what
She meant—imploring the goddess in that
Eastern dialect not to crush her but to help
Seduce the one she loved. Now, here she sits
In my backyard on this wet, summer afternoon,
Aphrodite in a white silk gown that conceals

Nothing. (A little damp and algae on a bench
Doesn't bother a sea-born goddess.) She brushes
The dried salt of the ocean out of her hair and
Laughs, "The throne is not always gleaming
Metal or the soft carpet of a panther's hide.
It's here nestled beside the overgrown hedge,
The air conditioning vent you never threw away,

The broken café table, random ferns, and orchids
Rotting like the wood where I sit, slats that
Leave red marks against my thighs—I saw you
Looking." "Aphrodite," I say, "I'm an old man now.
I have seen your bottom in front of Velazquez's
Mirror, and I did not look away then either."
She laughs again, admiring her own reflection

In the rainwater pooled by her bare feet.

"Beyond the Pleasure Principle"

Eros and Thanatos are this year's cute couple,
Shopping at IKEA for furniture they'll later
Put off assembling, eating Swedish meatballs
And apple cake in the café, drinking lots of coffee.
Eros wants to have children—someday—lingers
Besides the cribs and stuffed toys, the crayon sets,
And wooden puzzles. From downstairs, a baby
Makes a racket, causing Thanatos to grimace,
Less than enthusiastic about an infant crawling
On the carpet, extra loads in the washing machine.
In the parking lot, Eros forgets which level the car
Is on, so they wander through shadowy, concrete
Passages, pushing their cart heavy with poorly
Balanced boxes, with bags of kitchen gadgets they'll
Never use. Thanatos complains all the way home.

Orphic Mysteries

Orpheus sits at the bar of Outback Steakhouse.
He orders a sirloin medium rare and finishes it quickly,
Along with a potato and sour cream, bacon on the side.
His lyre rests by his feet because he wants to leave
The stool next to him open. Just because Eurydice's gone
For good doesn't mean someone else won't come along.
It's dark, so you'd struggle to see that he's not wearing pants,
Just a chiton tied at the waist and, because it's winter,
A length of wine-colored wool draped over his shoulders.
The woman who sits down grins and orders an old fashioned.
She asks if he's an actor in a show. Orpheus picks up
The lyre to work his magic, but the noise of plates and conversation
Is just too loud. He asks if she'd like to go outside, but that seems
A little fast under the circumstances. She demurs. The bartender
Considers alerting security, then holds off. A buzzer nearby
Starts to vibrate and flash a red light. Someone's table is ready,
But Orpheus doesn't know that. He makes for the door without
Paying and would have gotten there, but he trips over
A pair of legs waiting for a table, an old man who lets out
A scream as Orpheus falls. Two waiters drag him to his feet
And remind him about his unpaid check. After some discussion,
They take the lyre as collateral.

LUNCH IN HARTFORD

You watch the sky slip sideways like water,
The clouds sluicing toward inevitable ocean,
Afternoon the intricate gears of a medieval clock.
Martinis are an exercise in precision,
The olive's cruel toothpick pointing north
Toward tundra that's nothing like Connecticut,
Ice-colored pillowcases, honeymoon sheets.

You watch the sky and tell time by the wind—
See how it shifts at two o'clock—and drink
Until the sunlight slopes the cut-glass pitcher
And divides itself to patterns on the table.
In place of certainty, ritual, nodding to
A waiter you recognize, his jacket spotless
As the cool cheek of the woman you cannot kiss.

PASTICHE

Virginia Woolf swore she saw you in green make-up,
A widower whose wife was still alive, like James's American
Except you were the one sleeping in a church (the basement, or so

I like to imagine), your life turned embarrassment—which doesn't make
Sense really. *The Waste Land* had already let the wife out of the bag,
The chess partner who'd slept with Russell for marriage counseling.

You fled to church—who wouldn't have? Philosophy wasn't any more
Helpful to you than poetry was to Whitehead when his son died.
The world has so many ways to crush us. We retreat to maintaining

An appearance: a job, a well-tailored suit. It doesn't ease the hurt,
But fewer people see the wound. We're never who we wish we were.
Zoroaster met his image in the garden, but nothing changed. Celia

Dead in Kinkanja, lucky to have found a destiny. The rest of us
Don't have one and are only martyred by rich food, tobacco, or
Whatever there is to drink. You met your own image in magazines

And in the daily papers, a famous pair of glasses, a tall man with
A stoop—no more you than you were you, yourself your own ghost—
Yes, *familiar, compound,* identity that's suspiciously

Unreal in the mirror, or staring back from the Thames, oily and dark,
Blackout curtains on the windows, bombs that missed.
We still don't know what you really believed, how you imagined

Death or heaven, hell or personality. At Princeton, Paul Goodman
Pretended not to recognize you: "Sorry, didn't catch the name," he said.
"Eliot," you replied. "Tom Eliot."

.

IV.

The night stays chilly, the stars brighter.

Pat-down by the X-Ray Machine

At the prison where I teach, the guards
Never last very long. By the time
Buzzards migrate back in the fall and

Circle again over some roadkill,
They've left for a job with better pay.
The new ones dig with gloved fingers in

The pockets of my jacket, pull out
Tissues or Bic pens, then put them back,
And the guard patting me down forgets

To have me lift each foot to check my
Socks for contraband. It doesn't
Matter, though. I leave my money in

The car, next to my cell phone, and—no,
No weapons or drugs. I complain to
My students about how long it takes

To get in when there's a line or when
Shift changes. One laughs and reminds me,
"It takes a lot longer to get out."

Teaching Walt Whitman in a Prison in Florida

I thought of you, Walt Whitman, three summers ago,
When I stood on that hill in Brooklyn, looking down on the river,
Considering how you might be standing there as well,
Or under my boot-soles, except I wasn't wearing boots. Now,
I think of you again, this time in the parking lot of a prison
In the Everglades. If you were teaching my class here, what
Would you tell these students, so many
With life sentences, meaning they'll never leave?
One just wrote a love poem to a woman who'd died of Covid.
She'd corresponded with him for a while and then stopped.
He'd had Covid too and almost died. Most
Of my students had it more than once. The guards
Were contagious, dormitories unventilated. Not hard to see
How it spread. Walt, my students' loves are even
More remote than yours and their griefs certainly more private.
You would say you do not reject them, they and you are the same,
But, is that true? Their privacy is more like Dickinson,
Who didn't want to be advertised. When they grieve,
They don't want to be seen doing it. From that hill
In Sunset Park, I could see office buildings in Manhattan,
Boats on the river, but not the future, not like you.
Maybe I side with Dickinson here after all, believing
We're hidden nobodies, histories without selves. Some
Of my students are Buddhists and get up early to meditate.
Maybe they find it reassuring to imagine the self an illusion,
The razor wire on the fence just as unreal as the bodies they
Will someday leave—and the mind no more real
Than the body. But then, where do poems come from,
These words stacked on top of one another? Don't tell me
They come from the language. Language is circumstance, not
Will or intention, and there's nothing accidental about your words
Or anyone's. Stevens heard it as the will to order, but we never
Got around to him this semester, not enough time. We rushed toward
December, carrying copies of poems I'd printed and passed out.
By the end, there was a tall stack of them, Dickinson and Williams

On top of Ginsberg and you, Walt, your origins and theirs unresolved.
Then, the guard appeared to announce it was already 7:00 and time to
Line up, return to the dorms. Every week when I walked out the gate
And heard the metal lock clang into place, I felt happy,
Not just because I was leaving a prison but because I had
Carried those poems in with me, yours among them, spoken
And not spoken, like the kind of artifacts 19th century explorers
Brought back from islands, jungles, places where they hadn't
Understood how to ask for water or rice, where they would
Gesture to the bowl of milk being passed from hand to hand and
Pretend to drink. Sitting in my car, I look over the poems we
Read, rushing to get them in before 7, before the guard
And the line outside. Did we understand your isolation
Or Dickinson's brutal wit? Probably not. But the poems
Went back into the dormitories, into stagnant air,
Smells of sweat, illness, ramen noodles prepared with
Hot water from the sink. The students brought them back there,
Not artifacts of another world but evidence
Of a private one, their own.

EACH YEAR, WE CAME BACK

Turner was a realist after all, I thought.
The fog settled onto the lagoon, wake
Of the vaporetto smoothing behind us,
The sun's angle illuminating salt mist,
Making it glow with the end of daylight,
Glimpses of stone walls, clouds
Hanging on the water.

From the campanile in front of the basilica,
You can see mountains to the north, and
To the west, the plain of the Veneto. On top
Of the houses along the Giudecca canal,
There are places to sit and feel the earth
Pinball from one bumper to another.
To the east, the Balkans, Greece,
Turkey. To the south, Bologna and Rome.

There used to be a webcam in the San Marco.
I would stream it on my computer at work—
Crowds filing toward the steps or
Looking at the clock. Sometimes, I'd
Get lucky and catch that late afternoon
Light skirting the rooftops, gold on
Terracotta tiles.

I wanted to stand on the Academia bridge
And be happy, stupidly happy, to buy pastries
And blood oranges, to drink *vino novello*,
Wine they sell from barrels. You bring a plastic
Water bottle, and they fill it up. But, what's
About to go wrong never tells you in advance:
A wife secretly miserable, a son sad, friendless.
Each year, we came back until we didn't.

ACHILLES' VALET

Each time, I watched him chariot off
To battle, his armor properly

Polished, sword so sharp it could cut a
Fly in two. The horses' lips foamed white

Spit, caught by the wind, black hooves trampling
Shields, hands, the Trojan mud. He always

Came back happy, the filth of bodies,
Acid bile, and sweat hanging from him

Like perfume. I worked all night to clean
The stink while he made up songs on his

Lyre about his own greatness, how he
Made this one or that grovel at his

Sandals then killed him anyway—he
Never liked much taking prisoners—

And when he slept, Thetis would appear
To sit by his couch till dawn, stroking

With her pale hand his innocent head.

Sir Bedivere in Iowa

He should never have asked me to do it. What the gods have given, you don't give back. We hid in the marshes, last men crawling after that battle.

Then, in a low voice he told me to throw it into the night-stained waters of the lake. Twice I lied to him and said I'd done it, but I had no talent for deception.

He coughed and sent me back again. It was not the beauty or the sword's value made me hesitate or the memory of having fought beside him, having seen it wet with blood and those parts of a man that are better not seen. It was the ending presaged, abandonment of what had made our life worthwhile.

And the white hand that caught the hilt and dragged it back to hell or heaven or to whatever place it had been forged, that hand left nothing behind when it vanished beneath the unblinking surface of the mere.

I told the story later, in other lands, how a ship had skimmed the water's calm and carried Arthur off to sleep and heal.

It was a lie. I've gotten better at deception. I had no shovel for a grave and rolled his armored frame into the lake to ripen into something fish could chew and watched that body sink until the mud-soft bottom claimed it—

His gauntlet was the last of him I saw. Now, I sell insurance in Des Moines, drink beer with friends at an Irish sports bar on Sunday afternoons. Sometimes I order a second plate of wings, fill my mouth with foam and lager, and I'm almost tempted to tell them how Arthur killed the giant on Mont Saint Michel, hacking his bald and massive head away from the shoulders—

But I stop myself. They'd rather talk about football or whatever they heard last on Fox News. If nothing else, the price of real estate is a perennial favorite.

ECLIPSE

"Is it all the blood on the earth
Makes the shadow that color?"
She asks.
    —Kenneth Rexroth, "Blood on a Dead World"

Somewhere there is always a war.
Somewhere people are always dying of a disease
That could have been prevented or cured.
Somewhere the stars are shining oblivious
To whatever is happening here. Somewhere
Someone in a factory is cleaning out a vat of something
That requires protective gear that was never issued.
Somewhere someone always needs the work.
Tonight, there's a full lunar eclipse. It can be seen
From lots of places, and the parking lot outside
Is one of them. Somewhere the moon that turns
The color of drying blood reminds someone of a poem,
Just as it reminded me. Somewhere troops look though
Night goggles, watch the sky for drones or fighters.
By now the stars are a cruel joke. When the cities
Go black, stars shine even brighter than before.
If they were flashing messages, if they knew
Or cared, it would only be to tell us we don't matter.
If the universe has a center, it's not us. Light careens
Through the void without sentiment or purpose.
There was a poet whose four-year-old daughter asked if
The eclipsed moon was reflecting all the blood on earth.
But the earth just moves like one of those mechanical clocks
From the Middle Ages, clicking into place between the sun and
An orbiting ball of rock where nothing lives or grows.
Somewhere there is always a war, disputed territory,
Refugees in blankets, pink knitted hats, a plastic bottle with water.
Somewhere someone is always digging a grave or building
A funeral pyre out of furniture and broken boards.
Somewhere the earth's shadow crosses the moon.

APOLLO AND MARSYAS

On Ribera's canvas, Marsyas has already lost the contest.
His flute lies on the ground. The muse who'd judged god and mortal
Awarded the dark wreath and departed. What happened next was not
Her concern. Slowly, Apollo begins his work, tearing red strips

Of skin from Marsyas's leg. It will take a long time, but gods
Are patient. Marsyas's mouth is open and screaming. A set of pipes
Hangs motionless from a tree limb, an axeblade waiting to fall.
     The audience
Doesn't understand, and the god's face betrays nothing, neither horror

Nor pleasure, anger nor satisfaction. His cloak swirls and folds
In a wind of its own making. When Marsyas played, everyone danced,
But when Apollo took up his lyre, a calm entered their bodies. It was
Music that builds cities and creates constellations in the night sky.

Now, Apollo's hand separates the skin from bleeding flesh.
A body is just another instrument. He plucks the strings.

BELLINI'S *ANNUNCIATION*

Their faces are soft, both Mary's and Gabriel's.
Their hands touch the world as light touches objects,
Gently, without force. Gabriel holds a stalk of lilies,
And the Madonna, who is not yet the Madonna,
Rests one hand on the pages of a book, the other
Over her heart as though to remind herself
That it still beats. She hasn't noticed the angel.
He's entered as wind enters from a hallway,
His wings dark and heavy, his gray robe creased
And bent out of shape like armor after a battle.
Behind the Virgin, a landscape, buildings on a hill,
A lone cloud, some mountains drawn crudely. This
Is the world outside the painting, a world
Different from the one held in place by the angel,
The Madonna. Bellini says to us, "Choose. There
Is the dullness of a dream, a landscape painted
With indifference, and here is the moment of
Becoming—every detail sharper than your eye
Can comprehend, the blush on the Virgin's cheek,
The whiteness of her neck, the blue robe
That seems too large for her. What reality is
So real as these white lilies carried by the angel,
The fire-orange pollen that covers their stamens,
The angel's hair that flies above his shoulders,
The same color, the same fire?
In the time it takes to draw a breath, the Virgin
Will look up, the angel will speak. Quick,
Choose before it's too late."

On the Dogana's Steps

"I sat on the Dogana's steps
For the gondolas cost too much, that year...."
    —Ezra Pound, Canto III

I.   *A Small Apartment*

It was cheap to fly on New Year's Eve, the
Plane roaring through dark air, the sun left behind
Seven hours to the west, the invisible

Ocean laid out below, something we can't see
But believe exists. I forget how long
Ago that was. I only remember my

Son asleep in his seat, his headphones slipped
Down around his neck, the lemon peel I'd
Given him to fend off nausea falling

From his hand. Did we land at Zurich? Milan?
I forget that too. We were traveling to
Venice, a small apartment across from the

Opera house. Nothing was playing, but
The lights were on, and tourists would pack the
Square at dinnertime. There was the fish market

In the morning, gorgonzola dolce from
A shop nearby, and blood oranges on an
Old blue platter. At night, I walked with Simon

Through narrow streets to the San Marco, where
Venders sold mechanical toys and colored
Flashlights. You could still feed the pigeons then,

I think. Now, the police will give you a stern
Warning. I didn't know why I was there,
Browsing hand-blown glass and silk ties I couldn't

Afford. I slipped between pews of churches
And down stone stairs in galleries, searching
For Tiepolo angels and Bellini

Madonnas, Mantegna's *Saint Sebastian*.
I looked for Pound's grave in the cemetery
And leaned on the rail of vaporettos.

I stared at my reflection in the canal.

II.   *Acqua Alta*

This has been a year of destruction. Notre-Dame
Burned; now Venice floods. On the Giudecca,
Palladio built his church high above

The canal where lumbering cruise ships send
Their rough wakes crashing against the embankment,
The docks. Someday soon, it may be all that's

Left dry. I had a dream once like that: a drowned
City with only a few buildings standing
Above the water curling against their steps.

I was following a woman in that dream
Without success—an embarrassingly
Obvious reminder of wanting and need.

Today, the morning tide was more than a
Meter deep, climbing the stone steps of the
Basilica in the San Marco, seeping

In across the tiles, café tables and chairs
Washed away out to sea. The videos on
The news showed the flood but not the damage,

Floating suitcases, storefronts, and men in
Yellow slickers, rubber boots up to their thighs.
I think of places I've stayed, apartments where

The lagoon must have entered the living room,
Soaked the wallpaper and the furniture,
The bookshelves with histories of the Doges—

Art books ruined, stains that won't go away.

III.   Ruins

There are islands in the lagoon with ruins,
Collapsed houses, walls that turn red at sunset.
It's a mystery who lived here, why they left.

You pass these on the way to the airport.
Whoever built them, they wanted solitude
And must have had the money to purchase it.

On Torcello, there's a mosaic of the
Last Judgment that's just shy of a thousand
Years old and a white stone chair said to

Have been carved to fit Attila's rear end
When he chased the fleeing Romans across
These swampy islands. It's not true, but it's

A good story. Back in North America
Nothing is really old, except the caves
And the Indian mounds. It makes us think

History began with a few men in wigs
Deciding what to do with a continent.
It makes us think time is a harmless snake

With rings of bright color like a bracelet,
Only biting people who deserve it.
In Texas once, I found arrowheads by

The Guadalupe River and even a
Sharp wedge of flint that might have been part
Of an axe. I cut my thumb on the chipped edge.

I used to believe that if things turned bad, I
Could fly to Venice, live on coffee and
Polenta, sit somewhere on the Zattere,

And read all those books I've been meaning to
Get around to. Now, that seems unlikely.
The lagoon is taking back the palaces,

The churches, the narrow streets, ornate windows,
And the Dogana's steps, where Pound sat, host
Crabs and squid. On the roof of La Salute,

Baroque angels stare blankly at the waves.

    IV.   *Quarantena*

Palladio's church in the Giudecca
Was built by plague survivors. The Scuola
Di San Rocco was as well. Tintoretto

Spoke to that heaven prayers couldn't reach.
Doctors in black cloaks, drugs that didn't cure,
Left only this, paintings posed against death.

Simon, at four or five, played beneath the
Busy crucifixion, asked about the wounds—
Afterwards, coffee in the sunlight, the same

Sun that draped shadows five hundred years ago,
That made us squint as we crossed the canal.
The richest fled to their estates, burned herbs

And candles—transactions in the eternal
Ledger, this much gold, a painting to honor
The saint, the virgin, avoidance of this vice

Or another, faces carved in gray stone.
Ships from infected ports flew yellow flags
And waited forty days, *quarantena,*

Before they could dock. This summer no one
Is traveling. Our groceries are left
Outside the door, and masks are back in fashion.

The shopping mall down the street has reopened,
But there are few cars. The golf course is empty
Except for white ibises, Muscovy ducks.

I look up at the ceiling fan that doesn't
Work. There is no Tiepolo above me,
Full of gods and clouds, just wooden beams and

A roof, a narrow strip of sky dividing
The Atlantic from the Caribbean.
The sickness is getting closer. Simon's

Mother called to say she was being tested,
A sore throat that had lasted for days, shortness
Of breath. The hospital ICUs are full.

My great-aunt used to tell stories about
Quarantines, Spanish flu, the yellow fever
They had in Mississippi when she was

A child. She was very short, and my mother
Said yellow fever had stunted her growth,
Killed others. She used to warn me about

Night air. On the Lido, there's an old Jewish
Cemetery overgrown with vines, gravestones
Falling on top of each other, sinking

Beneath their own weight, Hebrew letters, carvings,
Two men with hats carrying grapes from a pole
Over their shoulders, a jug, a basin.

The dead will always outnumber the living.

—September 6, 2020

In Oak and Hickory

An old Ford abandoned in the woods
Where I walked my dog and watched for deer,
Trees grew around it, it couldn't leave.
Names were carved in oak and hickory.

When I walked my dog and watched for deer,
I could hear leaves stirred by unseen feet,
Names carved into oak and hickory,
Names carved thirty, forty years before.

I could hear leaves stirred by unseen feet,
Tree limbs shifting to let the light fall,
Names carved thirty, forty years before,
Worn like gravestones or memorials.

Tree limbs shifted to let the light fall
On the rusted body, collapsed wheels
Worn like gravestones or memorials.
They would have talked here till late at night,

By the rusted body, collapsed wheels,
Seats with broken springs, the damaged roof.
They would have talked here till late at night,
Frightened by owls, deer breaking cover,

On seats with broken springs, damaged roof,
Just room to stretch out on a blanket.
Frightened by owls, deer breaking cover,
Fears of the dark were eased by whiskey.

Just room to stretch out on a blanket,
Their pocketknives dulled by bark and sap,
Their fears of the dark eased by whiskey —
The night grew chilly, the stars brighter.

Their pocketknives were dulled by bark, sap.
Memory is sticky like that too.
The night stays chilly, the stars brighter.
Wars start in Korea, Vietnam.

Memory is sticky like that too.
Trees grow around it so it can't leave.
Wars start in Korea, Vietnam.
An old Ford's abandoned in the woods.

"Such was the funeral of Hector, breaker of horses."

Untouched by rot, Hector's ransomed body
Burns through the night, and in the morning, wrapped

In cloth, his brothers place the bones still warm
Inside a tomb. From the time Priam returns

To the wide gates, mourning takes only a page
Or two to recite. Helen recalls how kind

He was when others weren't. A feast follows.
Grief is collapsed, abbreviated. Homer

Says guards were posted. Achilles couldn't be trusted
To keep his word. The inhabitants of Troy

All know their war has died with Hector. Their
Homes and white bones will be just another layer

Of Turkish clay. Tourists will stare down
Into the excavation. Then air-conditioned

Buses will drive them back to their waiting ships.

ODYSSEUS

He was not a good man, not even
A good king, his kingdom just a rugged island,
Crops, some sheep, dogs, a few slaves. There's no
Record that he cared much for any of them—
Sheep, slaves, dogs, or even his wife. He slept
With goddesses and nymphs, or at least that's
What he said he did. We know him as storyteller,
Clever warrior, beloved by Athena and hated by
Poseidon. This is what happens when a man mixes
With gods, with monsters, when he travels off
To a long war after pretending to be mad to avoid it.
Usually, his tricks worked better than that, the Trojan
Horse or telling the cyclops his name was No Man.
Not *good* then, but certainly, *good at*. He found
Achilles hiding among the women, dressed
In some harem outfit. Apparently, there were other
Heroes not eager to waste ten years laying siege to
Troy. Then, when he returns, he and Telemachus
Butcher the suitors—read neighbors—who'd made
The mistake of thinking he was dead. Noblesse oblige
Wasn't something he'd been taught. Working-class
Thersites, who questioned Agamemnon, was lucky
To get off with only a beating. *Odysseus, old trickster,*
Why after so long do we still sit and listen, unless our story
Is really the same as yours, unless we, like you, want
More than anything to find our way home?

THE ASSASSINATION OF SAINT PETER MARTYR
—Giovanni Bellini, 1507

Saint Peter Martyr drops to the ground, writing
Credo in his own blood—the cleaver that cut
Into his skull made visible by restoration.
The assassin crouched above him finishes the job
With a plunged knife. His face in shadow has
Become indistinguishable from death itself.

He holds the saint's wrist with one hand as he
Stabs with the other. Behind them, time moves
Across the landscape the way sunlight crosses
The trees where the woodsmen will discover
The bloody sap of a miracle as they chop.

Through the foliage: sky and mountains, Milan,
Like heaven, too far away for help. The shepherds,
Woodcutters, dog, and livestock are scattered
To the future just as the friars' books are
Scattered on the sullied earth, blasphemy added
To murder—Bellini knew the rarity of books.

V.

I invented God in the late afternoon in October.

ALCESTIS

We can all agree: the husband wasn't worth the sacrifice.
When Death came to fetch her, he probably thought
Something similar and must have been tempted to give her up
To Heracles without a fight. Still, principles are principles,
And he went ahead with the wrestling match. Heracles
Was still a bit drunk, but truth be told, Death doesn't
Wrestle very well. The big guys are usually not a problem.
Either they're keeled over on the toilet like Elvis, or they're
Too depressed to struggle—old football injuries and concussions
Take their toll. But Death put up a good fight that time.
He knew this one would be talked about, one way or the other,
And he didn't want the Fates making quiet, ironic jokes
As they cut the thread of some fisherman's or baker's life:
Death, do you think you can handle this one? Some people
Say he even cheated a little, pulling the demigod's long
Hair, trying for a kick down below—none of it worked.
And all the time, Alcestis' spirit lay there watching. Her face
Betrayed no sign of interest. If she grieved at giving up her life,
She didn't show it. Perhaps, she could already see herself walking
The banks of Lethe, then drinking deep to forget she had ever married.

FUNERAL RITES

I told my oldest son that I wanted my ashes
Dumped off the back of a vaporetto when none
Of the crew was looking, maybe somewhere
Between Fondamenta Nove and Murano.
I thought of myself floating slowly down into
The Venetian lagoon as fish opened their
Mouths to swallow flecks of human ash,
And whatever wasn't eaten mixing with
Mud and sand, algae, and twisted seaweed.
I imagine him afterwards wondering what
To do with the jar that had held the ashes.
Throw it away, or take it back to New Jersey
In his suitcase? Would this present a problem
At customs? Would smears of me and grains
Of unburned bone still cling to the inside?
Maybe he should dump the jar as well, but
It would be more obvious, perhaps a muffled
Thump as it hit the water. Drawing unwanted
Attention would be no help to anyone. Finally,
He decides to chance it, and just drops the
Container somewhere before the second stop
On Murano. He gets off there, goes for a short
Walk, looking for the iron bridge and the restaurant
Where we went for risotto and fried calamari.
But now, that restaurant either isn't there anymore
Or he's missed it, and it's starting to rain. So, he
Catches another vaporetto and goes back
To a stop he recognizes. The rain will have
Let up by then, I hope, and he'll find a café
And order a *caffè corretto* in my honor, feeling
The warmth of espresso and grappa as it
Reaches all the way to his stomach and his
Wind-chilled hands.

Act VI

In another play, Hamlet would have
Survived the duel, killed Claudius
And become king. Then, he'd have had to
Fight Fortinbras, who probably would
Have stuck a sword right through his entrails,
But let's assume he survived that one
Too and captured Fortinbras—then by
Necessity had to execute
The Polish prince. History would have
Demanded that sacrifice of his
Conscience, and you can see how quickly
Hamlet would have become his father.

A Brief Introduction

Anonymous wrote before writing existed,
Before figures on walls or scratches on papyrus,
Before prizes awarded at festivals, or
Fees for commemorating a charioteer.
Anonymous' works were voluminous and
Incomparable for their range of emotion
And varying topics, for their insight into a
Condition that wasn't quite yet human,
Horses and lions on the savanna, the night
Someone invented fire. Legend has it, he may
Even have been immortal—his works written
Over centuries, lifetimes spent on revision.
Anonymous carved letters into steles
Set up at the last hilltop before the desert
Began, warning travelers that beyond these
Words lay nothing but sand and empty sky.
Anonymous satirized the emperor and the court,
Describing their sexual encounters in precise
Detail, how this one needed tincture of
Rhinoceros sperm to get an erection and that one
Was so dry she filled herself with an amphora
Of olive oil before each assignation. Thus,
Anonymous often found it necessary to flee
From one country to another, and his works
Became full of travel, prison, and escapes
Over rooftops. Sometimes Anonymous bunked
In sour hay with pigs and goats and sometimes slept
In Chinese silk or cotton from Egypt. The works
Of Anonymous have been praised by both
Grammarians from Alexandria and the harshest
Critics of medieval Baghdad. Yet despite these
Accolades and the evidence, prima facie, of
The texts themselves, some lesser scholars
Still persist in doubting his existence.

The Idol-Maker's Prayer

My Gods, you lie smashed on the stones.
Here is an arm, and here wings, here
A beard, a face broken to pieces. It was
My own son, Abram, who did this thing
Without thought of the results, the heavy
Breasts of the goddess in shards, the harvest
That may never arrive again. I am shamed
Before my city, before the neighbors
Who look away, too frightened yet
To be angry, to burn my house,
Kill even the livestock for this blasphemy.
Gods of Ur, forgive Abram for what he
Has done, forgive him also for lying
To taunt the righteous, for claiming you
Fought among yourselves. Although his hair
Is gray and his skin dried by sun and wind,
He is still a shallow boy and thinks that because
Your images do not move or talk that they are
Somehow false. He says that an invisible
God speaks to him, one without a name or face,
As though an invisible god were more real
Than one crafted from the stones of a mountain
Or molded from the rich red clay of the Euphrates.
Even broken and desecrated, your forms
Call out to me, mourn the age that is ending,
Despair of what will happen to your faithful.
I will gather up all the sharp-edged pieces,
All the dust of your broken forms, and bury you
Secretly, at night without witnesses except
The stars and the moon or pale clouds that may
Cover the sky ashamed. Abram understands
None of this. I taught him to carve and to shape.
He had a good hand, but he prefers to stay with
The sheep in high pastures. He wants to travel
West or south, to leave Ur. His god has promised
Him a new land, and he wants me to leave as well.

Now, I will have to go with him. Who here would
Trust me again to make a true image of a god?
And you, my broken ones, will no longer protect
Me or this house where such a thing could happen.
There is no penance or sacrifice I could make
To bring you back. Now, I will have to go with him
And even offer a young goat to his invisible god
And make promises also. *Keep us safe, Imageless One.*
Do not shatter Abram's hopes as he shattered
The faces of the gods I molded and oiled. Keep us
Safe, and I will make you a beautiful idol
Out of the finest clay in the new land. You will
Tell me how to shape your face, and I will follow
As you guide my hand. I will keep you secret,
Hidden in my tent, and protect you against
My son's impetuous nature.

A History of Imperfection

In a few days, there will be an eclipse. The moon
Will move in front of the sun, and a hole will
Open in the blue weave of the sky, proving

Even God makes mistakes. No wonder the ancients
Were terrified. It is easy to praise imperfection.
There is so much of it around us and in us. We're

Flattered to hear the standards are not so high
As we were taught. But, between ourselves,
We know it's cheating. Awareness of imperfection

Haunts us like the ghost of an embarrassing uncle
Who was never invited to family meals. His revenge
Is persistence, rattling spoons in the cupboard,

Causing the air conditioning to falter on hot days.
"Sure, make a joke of it," he says, "but aren't there
Things you wish you'd said and didn't, and things

Your mouth should never have opened to say?"
We tell him he's right and hope he'll fall asleep
Before he gets specific, knowing better than he does

The gnawing culpability that sours wine and
Burns bread in the oven, apologies that restore
Our self-regard but can't undo anything. Even the

Garden of Eden didn't last. The first mistake sent it
Tumbling to Earth and with it…. But, from there
The story gets it wrong. Adam, useless, blamed God

And everyone but himself, while Eve, our mother,
Had to give birth alone to three children. One she
Called *Memory*, another *Desire*, and the third *Shame*.

THE DAY I INVENTED GOD

I invented God in the late afternoon in October. The light came in at an angle through the pine trees, and someone was making dinner.

I invented God on a day in October, not long after my grandfather died.

My grandfather had collapsed the way they imploded the old casinos in Atlantic City: first, the sound of explosives, and then, the building crumbling in on top of itself. Where it had stood, rubble and dust, a sense of something missing, a hemorrhage.

I invented God on a day in October when I was seven or eight years old. I knew the story where he called out to Samuel in the middle of the night, and I decided he should have my grandfather's voice. Later, I discovered I could talk as much as I liked. He would never reply, never stop me in mid-sentence to tell me I had it wrong. And, if he reprimanded, it was only my own voice, assuming what he would say if he were going to say it. Eventually, I forgot what my grandfather's voice sounded like, and I never heard it coming from him.

That afternoon in October, I was sitting on the red brick steps outside the house, trying to remember my grandmother who'd died before I could speak and a great aunt who'd lived in New Mexico. Nobody bothered me at times like that. I got as far as remembering my great aunt's room when she was sick, that it was green and the shades were drawn. My mother had taken me to visit when I was so young that memory and what I'd been told were mixed together.

I invented God in the late afternoon in October. The light came in at an angle through the pine trees, and someone was making dinner.

What Dying Is Like

My oldest son tells me my poems make him sad.
I tell him they do the same to me.
I think too much about my own parents,
How their lives ended in sheets changed
By nurses, blue pads soaked with urine,
In caregivers who locked themselves out
Of the house by accident, decubitus ulcers,
My father's swollen belly, bone-shrunk face,
My mother's clenched hands, frozen elbows.
For a while, a woman tended her who claimed
To understand each mumbled phrase. *She says
She wants her milkshake now.* It wasn't true,
But I lived in Boston, not Louisiana. Finding
People to care for her wasn't easy.
The same woman brought a teddy bear
And posed it in the crook of my mother's arm.
She loves her teddy bear.
It made me angry to see it, but I didn't say anything.
If treating her like an infant made it easier, there
Wasn't much to do about it, and by then,
My mother didn't recognize anyone.

Afternoon in November

I've grown used to disappearing—not
Being here anymore as me, that
Sequence of whatever stories I
Tell myself to create a person.
There, in each other's arms, stories stop,
Thought ends, the way it ends in air-blue
Emptiness, the ragged edges of
White clouds becoming transparent, leaves
Shuffled against leaves, invisible
Wind, buzzards circling hundreds of feet
Above the ranch-style houses, asphalt
Driveways, streets that twist back and emerge
Into the fast flow of traffic south
Or west, toward fields green with tomato
Vines and strawberries, tangled thorns of
Bougainville, shallow marshes that
Somewhere become ocean. The buzzards
Don't see me, sitting by the window,
Staring up at heavy coconuts
Clustered together, fronds and tree limbs
Moving at the same time, some almost
Imperceptibly, and if I look
Hard, I won't see myself in any
Of this either. The tree limbs and sky
Will still be there, the buzzards too, but
I won't exist as an audience.
This morning in the kitchen, it was
The same. I kissed that spot where your neck
And shoulder meet and lost myself in
The scent of bath soap, of dark coffee.

IN THE AFTERLIFE

If Lew Welch met Kafka in the afterlife,
Would they sit over coffee with cream and
Discuss cockroaches? Would Welch confess
To writing, "Raid kills bugs dead!" Gregor
Samsa might have something to say to that.
So, I think Welch would talk instead about
Lichen in the High Sierra, what it feels like to
Pass the tree line, the hardness of rock, how the
Wind seems to snake around mountains. Kafka
Would remember Prague, the pastry shops,
The shuls, the men pulling carts on the street.
He'd ask if Welch had ever been downwind
Of a brewery in the morning, sour odor of grain
Fermenting in vats, or looked down on a medieval
City asleep and wondered where they all find
The confidence to rest, to shut their eyes and
Pull their duvets up to their chins and ears. Do
They know something we don't, he might ask?
Does an angel hide beneath their beds, protecting
Them against the great wheel rolling toward
Their houses and their desks, crushing their favorite
Table at the café, breaking a dog's ribcage, smashing
The opera house and the promenade, reducing
Linden trees to splinters? Welch would say no.
San Francisco, Chicago, Prague are all the same
In the last hours of night, shutters unrattled by
Wind or rumors. The fire escapes are Jacob's ladders
Leading to whatever it is that can't be known. They
Are blacker than the void of darkened windows, and
Welch would invite Franz to climb one with him,
Or go for a walk in the mountains.

VI.

The rapid clicks that sounded like rain.

SCIENCE FICTION IN CANTON PALACE

In Canton Palace, a waitress coughs
As she sweeps the carpet. I look up
From my plate of rice and fish. It's nine
O'clock, the end of the evening. Tea
Steams in the cup. My son Simon has
Finished his noodles. We've been talking
About plot and scenes, exposition,
The elements he's been working on.
I say how strange it is that people
Will pay money for stories. The same
Money that buys food and cars, laptops
And refrigerators, they'll spend to
Read a tale set on a planet with
Two suns and three moons, characters not
Quite human, obsidian mountains,
And deserts where blue-red flames explode
Into a cold, unbreathable sky.
The protagonist wishes he could
Save everyone, but nothing works out.
Characters die—a few will survive,
Not necessarily the noblest
Or the smartest. A good writer knows
Darwin was wrong. It's the luckiest
Who'll make it through another chapter.
I put down my chopsticks and look out
The window. Simon is already
Walking outside, past the bakery,
Cellphone store, empty parking spaces.
He's figuring out what happens next.

GHOSTS

The bathroom mirror shows them to me—
Not complete as they were in life but
Fragments, an expression, nose at a
Certain angle, hairline retreating.
Often, I'll repeat something that my
Mother said, shrug like my grandfather,
Talk to myself as I shave like my
Father did. In a cemetery
In Louisiana, their coffins
Must have collapsed by now beneath the
Weight of wet soil and clay, but here they
Are, inhabiting me, without an
Invitation. I frown the way I
Did at the breakfast table with the
Green cover in my parents' bedroom.
I'd toss back dry toast and orange juice
While my father made coffee in a
Percolator. It smelled burnt and sour,
Undrinkable. I hated school and
In the evenings prowled through old issues
Of The National Geographic,
Imagining myself cycling down
Canal paths in France, dressed in a black
Turtleneck, eating sausages and
Baguettes. It didn't work out that way,
But my parents and I were used to
Disappointing ourselves, each other.
I wash soap bubbles, flecks of whiskers,
Off my chin and reach for a towel.

Real Monsters

In *Forbidden Planet*, the monster
Was Walter Pidgeon's Freudian *id*,
A less-eloquent Prospero bent
On attacking those space sailors who'd
Take his daughter back to Earth. It was
Invisible, as the scariest
Terrors sometimes are. *My beloved
Is mine as rooms are empty*, Auden
Might have written but didn't. The worst
Monsters take the form of absence. In
Fritz Lang's *M*, the child's ball rolls away,
Each black-and-white bounce more horrible
Than the last. By contrast, Frankenstein's
Creature is touchingly innocent.
Fleeing from his own ugliness, he
Accidentally commits his crimes.
He inspires pity but also, like
His creator, we wish him elsewhere.
Real monsters are deliberately
Evil, whether dressed as white-faced clowns
Or smiling presidents with cufflinks
And cologne—or perhaps appearing
As normal folks, not too young or old,
The man who trims his hedge on weekends,
The wife with chocolate chip cookies,
Photographed in front of a garage,
Waving to the camera and by
Extension us, the helpless viewers:
Welcome! Come in. Please stay for dinner.

AT THE NEXT TABLE

At the next table, a woman is drinking tea,
A gray sweater over the back of her chair,
Her face turned toward a large mirror behind
The counter, the back and forth of waiters,

The door to the kitchen opening, swinging shut.
For the last twenty minutes, I've tried to read
A book I don't love—it's won awards, and
Important writers write how important it is.

Each time I reach the end of a page, I stop
And let my eyes drift toward the pipes that
Run across the ceiling. Her head bends forward
A little whenever she lifts her cup. From where

I'm sitting, I can see brown hair touching
Her shoulders. I turn the page—the narrator
Is still narrating, and I'm well into the book.
No one else has made an appearance.

Out on the sidewalk, rain darkens the pavement,
Matching the color of her sweater.

"Watermelon Man"

I'm so used to interrogating happiness,
Mistrusting the deep breath I take looking
At green treetops, sky, clouds just passing through—
It's hard to imagine what Freddie Hubbard must
Have felt on that track, trumpet flying,
His certainty where the notes were going to land.
Maybe I dwell on loss so much only because
It's easier than this, because music doesn't translate,
Because words can't contain Dexter Gordon
And Hubbard, because I can't describe the feeling of
A bird's shadow crossing the wooden boards of a fence
Or tree limbs full of leaves moving in time with
Hancock as he touches the keys of a piano.

"Ain't Nobody's Business"

It's a rainy Sunday afternoon,
Trees thrashing heavy green limbs against
The sky—unbroken gray. I'm playing
Jimmy Witherspoon, recorded at
Monterey in 1959,
Singing blues with so much happiness
It defies reason—probably just
What it's supposed to do. The streets are
Too wet for walking in sneakers, and
My jeans would get soaked even if I
Took an umbrella. There's a long roll
Of thunder, and I look west over
The fence to see if there's any chance
The sky will clear by sunset. The rain
Has let up a little. Palm fronds are
Dripping now onto stacked bricks and tiles,
Moving in quiet conversation
With the oak trees. The clouds turn a shade
Of dark violet mixed with rose, and
A long streak of sky opens over
Hedges, rooftops. I put on my shoes.

Muscovy Ducks

At winter solstice, canals should be slow moving,
Not a brown surge of water clambering banks,
Rustling the noon-white sun in its reflection.
Muscovy ducks reconnoiter the parking lots,

Retreat beneath oaks and sea grape, leaning
Over to jab quickly at palmetto bugs
Or maybe bread I throw in their direction.
By now, they know me, look up as I arrive.

Some, fearful, flap to roost on the golf course,
Its lake also uncommonly high, reptiles
Twisting beneath the surface, slaloming
The weeds. But most would rather take their chances

Pecking at curtilage, gravel, and roots of trees.
Yesterday, one was broken limbs and feathers,
Lopsided by the curb. I smelled the carcass,
Saw it, and hardly knew it was a bird.

HEISENBERG IN THE SUBURBS

Last night, I threw apples out back for
The possums, or maybe the rats. You
Can never know which will find them first.
The apples were the green kind and had
Stayed on the table too long, their skins
Dry and wrinkly. In the dark, I threw
Them in the direction of the fence.
The grass is high over there, the vines
Untrimmed. I don't know where they landed.
Throwing an apple in the dark is
An exercise in uncertainty.
You never know what will find it or
What trouble you might be causing. I
Remember getting a call one day
That the backyard was full of huge birds.
My Doberman killed a snake, I guess,
And then may have killed a raccoon or
Possum—by then, it was hard to tell
Which—that was trying to eat the snake.
Some buzzards got wind of this and packed
The yard, angling between themselves for
A shred of whatever was still left.
The dog did have a long history
Of snake-killing, but whatever was
Eating the snake might have killed it just
As easily, then choked on what he
Swallowed, and the poor dog barking at
The door may have played no part in it.
The buzzards weren't even curious.

ILLEGIBLE

The sky its usual blue, clouds peeling
Off, abandoned in the afternoon air—
Whatever you had to say, has been said
Already, and then again. Green letters
Drop from the branches, addressed to someone
Who no longer lives here. The post office
Will not forward them. Their ink fades onto
The squares of pavement, dries invisible,
Like messages spies send to each other:
Tell Mother we enjoyed the chocolates.
Send photos of the baby taking her
First steps. It's all in code, the sunlight slant
Against the fence, the gray wood in shadow,
The noise of a plane passing to the east.

A Lesson

Once I had the effrontery to tell my grandfather
That the ketchup bottle on the dining-room table
Was mine, and he got up out of his seat and slapped
Me hard. I was seven years old, and he was going
Senile—but I didn't know that. Neither did my friend
David, who was over for dinner and maybe more scared
Than I was. I remember staring at my mother, waiting
For her to say something, to tell her father we were
Leaving or even that she had bought that ketchup
At the supermarket because I'd asked for it,
But she just sat there, paralyzed by some mixture
Of emotions she never explained. I ran into the living room
While my grandfather finished dinner. That night,
There was roast beef and potatoes on my grandfather's
Table and big pitchers of iced tea with mint. His starched
Shirt was spotless, and he was wearing a Chinese silk tie.
He looked the same as always, and the silverware
And porcelain were the same as well. The overhead fan
Never stopped spinning. When he died a year later,
I admit I felt nothing.

Morse Code

Today it rained most of the morning
And afternoon—at first, a drenching,
Staticky sound on the roof tiles and
The broken crash of water sliding
Down the gutters, then the electric
Clicks of Morse code reminding me of
Radio sets and antennae made
Of copper wire looped and strung above
The driveway. I listened to broadcasts
In unidentified languages
But never got the license to send
Messages myself. Maybe I was
Too lazy to learn Morse and basic
Radio tech, or maybe I feared
The mystery would go out of it,
The voices I didn't understand,
The rapid clicks that sounded like rain.

VII.

I wasn't dying. Your white shoulders proved it.

VISITORS

Shreveport, Louisiana, 1961

On Sundays, we'd visit my grandmother's
Grave, bringing fresh flowers, pulling out
Weeds. The headstone was pink marble

With blue veins visible under the dates and
Carved letters. We swept oak leaves into
A brown pile for the trashcan, along with

Cigarette butts and crinkled cellophane.
Then, I'd go for a walk, looking for names I
Recognized: my grandmother's brother who'd

Died of lung cancer when I was five, my
Grandfather's sister who was a recent arrival—
We used to stop by her house two or three

Evenings a week. My mother told me she'd
Had strokes, *a vegetable*, but my grandfather
Thought she understood him and would sit

By her bed reciting whatever pieces of news
Might interest her. I never heard her reply, but
I didn't wait long either. I would go out front

To the square of lawn between house and
Sidewalk, lie flat on my back—dry, neatly
Cut grass rubbing my neck—and I'd look

At the moon rising over the line of houses
On Monrovia Street and the clusters of stars
That meant nothing to me, except they were far

Away and each night seemed to be different.

FAMILY LETTERS

Sheets of his stationery lay scattered on the floor.
A leather box rested with one corner dangling
Over the edge of the desk. There were fountain pens

With silver nibs and clean, thick sheets of paper,
Pens that had traced sweeping lines, the shape of words,
Of sentences etched onto the page, that began, "My Dear ..."

And ended with an embrace, a signature, a point where
Words stopped, folded against each other. If I'd had
My grandfather's handwriting, I'd also have used reams

Of paper and bottles of ink, worn out the nibs of pen
After pen, writing letters to be kept but lie unread
By those to whom they no longer mattered.

In my hand, though, pens have always wanted to escape,
The letters jerk, blot, or even collapse, each a jumble,
Something regrettable. My teachers told me

I should practice, but they never said why.
My parents are buried near an oak tree, next to the graves
Of my grandparents and my aunt. The stones are

Pink marble with blue veins running underneath
The inscriptions. My father's parents are buried
Somewhere else. They died when he was still a child.

I don't know their graves. But, I remember my
Father's monologues as he shaved, the dog asleep
At the foot of the bed, my mother's shout when my

Grandfather had a stroke, footsteps rushing downstairs.
I am older now than my mother was then, or my father.
I stood by my father's pillows when he died almost

Thirty years later, in a room that used to be mine,
My books still on the shelves, the carpet the same,
The same armoire against the far wall, a television, a desk.

He was faced toward the ceiling, and whatever he saw
Was not the room where I stood and he waited.
My mother was in the bedroom on the other side

Of the house, unable to feed herself, walk, or use
A toilet. I don't know what room she saw either, what
She remembered or had forgotten. We were, all three,

Unable to say anything then that mattered. Afterwards,
I found the boxes of papers, letters my grandfather
Wrote to my mother, letters my parents wrote to each other.

I sat on the floor of my mother's dressing room,
Reading my grandfather's studied hand, my mother's
Cautious script, and my father's large, scribbled lines,

But they told me nothing I didn't know already.
My grandfather wanted my mother to return from France.
My father missed my mother, was somewhere on business,

His handwriting on hotel stationery. These letters still
Exist, somewhere in a box at the bottom of my closet.
I've never known what to do with them, what to write in reply.

In the Last Days of an Empire

My son's in the kitchen making breakfast,
Pouring shots of espresso into his chocolate milk.
The sun has finally come out after a morning
Of rain, and now it cuts across the backyard
Past overgrown green bushes and variegated vines,
Filtered through the branches of black olive trees,
A shining liquid dripping onto the roof and the gray
Stained boards of the fence. Whatever else Simon
Prepared, he's disappeared with it into his room.
I've never known if I'm a good father. I've always
Let my children do what they wanted. My oldest
DJ'd through his teens all over Massachusetts, driving
At night with vans of equipment past triple-decker
Neighborhoods where the porch lights had already
Gone dark. My daughter headed off to France as
Soon as possible. Now, she's in Brooklyn, with her own
Child, writing short stories, poems. We commiserate
About rejections from magazines. Simon emerges
To tell me he's finished the third episode of his
Space-opera-slash-anime-slash-superhero-fiction.
I try to pretend I'm not too old to understand
What that means. It's unlikely any of my children
Will become rich. They're all too much like me, with
Too many other things to do with their lives. The golf
Course next door closed last spring with the Covid
Shutdown and hasn't reopened. It's been taken over by
Birds, flocks of ibises, ducks, trees filled with crows.
Right now, they're enjoying the afternoon sunlight,
The ponds still cool from the storm this morning, and
The quiet that comes with not giving a damn.

—September 30, 2020

In the Middle of Our Life

I woke up sweating, right foot tingling, the one
That couldn't tell hot from cold after the stroke.
But that was five, six years ago. Now, I

Mostly don't notice. Tossed off the blanket, trying
Not to wake up entirely, just check whether
I was still alive, awake enough to see

Your white shoulders rise above the pillow.
I felt too warm to hold you, go back to sleep
Kissing your neck or hair, but I knew by then

I wasn't dying. Your white shoulders proved it.

A CONFESSION

There are days I pretend I have nothing to do,
No documents to prepare or bills to pay,
No appointments requiring me to jump in the car

And drive across town, to curse the traffic when
Someone crosses slowly into the left-hand lane.
There are days I pretend I have read every

Book on my bookshelves, that the encyclopedia
Holds no more interest, that the dictionary's filled
Only with superfluous adjectives, with words

I'm unlikely to need, at least for a while. On that
Kind of day, I make myself an equally
Superfluous cup of coffee, having already

Had one at breakfast, and stand by the sliding-glass
Door, staring at the clouds' slow progression
Toward the Atlantic, the umbrella tree hanging

Leaf-heavy and quiet, and one of a dozen
Backyard lizards inflating his red throat
Before thinking better of it and pretending

He's part of a chair. On that kind of day,
Pretending is not so bad. I'm really no more
Superfluous than my neighbors, than the man

Who drives the blue recycling truck or
Or the real estate agent with the pink Cadillac,
But on days like this, I can accept that the world

Does not require me, that no one will mind
If I spend today like a lizard, pretending
To be indistinguishable from the foliage

And furniture, accomplishing nothing.

FAILED TRAJECTORIES

There were a record number of golf balls
Hidden in high grasses in the side yard
This afternoon, as I walked, chatting on

The phone, tossing them back on the fairway.
I think sometimes they aim for the west wall
Of the house, roof, or anywhere except

The goddamn ninth hole. I'm used to it now,
Though. In the morning, tractors trim the rough
Along the fence. My dog barks at them if

He's out. Someone will comb the sand trap with
A rake or move the hole up a little
Or down. Then, the golfers arrive in carts

That move like toys across the grass. I hear
Them swearing when they miss a putt, or over-
Shoot altogether green and flag, bouncing

Off asphalt drive or chain-link fence, their clubs
Held in the air as though they could pull back
The ball, the way fingers reset a clock

Until hour, day, or lifetime never happened.

A Walk at Dusk

Quick sunset bends the oak trees into twilight,
Crepuscular breezes, golfers returning home.
The neighbor's Mercedes, windows rolled, and some
Figures on balconies, rusted ochre, white,
Squint at low hedges and a face-down gnome.
Mapping in squawks a sharp ascending flight,
Disordered geese, unflocked, wing-clamber night.
Below, mute fire ants tunnel the humid loam.

This green sphere is a middle realm despite
Nietzschean aspirations, or republican Rome.
Who reads by oscillating candlelight?
Nostalgie de la boue, the courtesan's comb,
Are relics, an older century's fistfight
With God or suburb. The golfers have all gone home.

Written on Papyrus

Sky like the ocean, cyan going
To blue. I walk without looking up.
The sun must have followed the pavement
Past shop windows stocked with machines of
All sizes and design: the ancient
Singer that belonged to my mother.
Powered by pedals—it stood on an
Iron frame. My father's Pontiac:
Through the window, his sunglasses on
The dashboard—there's a price tag hung from
The door handle. Next, a lunch counter
With revolving stools and on each a
Dead relative, Cousin Mary and
Her husband who sold stationery—
Another who was allergic to
Clams, collapsed on the neatly mopped floor.
A bank opens onto dense forest,
Behind the teller's cages, pine trees
And feral cats rubbing against the
Bark, resin sticking to their fur, claws
Scraping against the wood. I head to
The bus station, knowing there's plenty
Of time. The river is so shallow
You could walk across on the sandbars.
Neon tubes flicker before sunset.
On the movie theater's marquee,
Too many black letters have been lost.
No one will ever know what they said.

A Visit Home

My cousin's company had installed
The electrical wiring for a
Riverboat casino down the hill
From where the bus station used to be,
A short walk from the Texas Street Bridge.
The "boat" was built on concrete pilings,
But regulations required it still
Have a captain, maybe even a
River pilot, I didn't find out.
I got the grand tour, though, the wheelhouse
All the way to the restaurant that
Served Surf 'n Turf to pull in farmers
And their families—the slot machines
And tables whispering in their ears.
There were men in white cowboy shirts with
Mother-of-pearl buttons and women
Who'd had their hair and nails done for the
Occasion. Some brought their toddlers and
Sleeping babies. Up the street there was
Larry Flynt's Hustler Club, its neon
Sign flashing $10 lap dances.
This was the entertainment district,
Which is enough, I think, to make a
Guy question whether capitalism
Isn't what the Marxists say it is.

July

Half the year is already gone. Maybe I
Wasted it—I'm not sure how you tell.
The buzzards who float in the wind above Miami
Won't be back until October. I read somewhere
They summer in Ohio, like the retirees from
New York, who used to winter on
South Beach in the residential hotels that are all
Torn down now. I used to see them sitting
Outside in those white metal chairs
That nobody bothered to steal. This was
The payoff for a lifetime of work standing
Behind a glass counter where customers
Didn't let them forget that whatever they
Were selling wasn't worth it. At the end of
Each day, they'd punch their timecards and take
The subway home, their ears used to the
Noise, and their eyes turned somewhere inside.
On the beach, their hotels, pastel colored, didn't
Even face the water, but they'd watch the sun
Set over the trees and apartment buildings.
As the sky darkened, they'd stand up, one at a time,
Drift inside to television or bed, the way the buzzards
In winter will let the warm air lift and carry them
As their sharp eyes scan the causeways and parking lots,
Rooftops and twisting streets.

For a Friend Who Looks Out Hospital Windows

The long sunsets at this time of year are not lost on you,
Or the thick green of treetops, though from up there
It might be hard to tell which are oaks and which are beech.
Some canopies cover the sidewalks and stretch across the narrow
Street, the intersection with its freshly painted lines. Far away,
A view of the river may slide between buildings, the pilings
Of a bridge, the barge passing quickly—It makes you
Think of Whitman until a speaker somewhere pages a doctor
Whose name might be important. Nurses are checking vitals,
Asking patients for date of birth. You've written about the smell of
The hallways, taken pictures of the light reflecting off the floors,
Metal fixtures. No one who doesn't work here should know
Such a place so well, should recognize the sound of a lunch cart
Or the low hiss of the air conditioning at night when it's quiet.
You didn't ask for that knowledge. No one does. Even though
They're all trying to help, even though the building itself
Is purposed for saving lives, pulling people back whose bodies
Have already resigned themselves to an emptiness where words
Stop meaning anything, where eyelids are almost still, even though
You're grateful for the monitors and tubes, the attention of nurses,
The rubbery squeak of their shoes before they knock and open the door,
Grateful for the charts, thermometers, and felt-tip markers
That are proof of life, of the possibility of a return to a time
When you could believe that everyone you loved was immortal,
That each nonsensical moment was separate, eternal—a series
Of photographs hung on a white immaculate wall, music
You heard driving here, songs linked to cities where you lived
Or worked, to the kind of arguments you had with friends as a kid,
About drummers or guitarists, about what made the chili so good
At one café or the peach pie at another—even though this is all true,
Even though memory and prayer might be the same thing,
The fluorescent light above the bed refuses to accept it.
The obscure color of the bathroom tiles (brown, beige, pink,
That stupid crayon color that used to be called flesh) says no,

Says there is only this world: Styrofoam cups and crushed ice,
Medication schedules and paper towels. That's when you look out
The window again, even if it's dark and you can only see streetlights
And the moon setting behind a hillside. Memory weighs more than
Styrofoam, more than an IV tube or an ugly blanket. Each breath
Has happened and can't be undone by the body's fatigue, by
A faltering heart. Stevens was right, despite working for that
Insurance company. Trust the "violence from within that protects us
From a violence without." Believe it protects against the smell of
Disinfectant and the static view from hospital windows,
From the cautious diction of prognosis, the weak coffee and
Powdered creamer you bring back from the cafeteria, from the pale
Light of your cellphone as you read in the dark. Push back
Against it all, and don't worry about what's true and what's imagined.
The brief touch of fingers, remembered scent of hair or skin, the light
That sloped through the window in the morning on a weekend are
A liturgy, repeated and real. Memory and prayer *are* the same thing.
Each breath happened and goes on happening. Light from the window
Illuminates the uncomfortable chair, the blanket.

VIII.

We don't know who is safe and who isn't.

SATURDAY

Across the street, a young woman and a middle-
Aged man are turned away from each other,
Each texting on their phones. It is easy to mock this.
But the woman is wearing jeans and a pink t-shirt,
And she has brushed her hair carefully, to make
A good impression on someone. The man's shirt
Is blue, and he moves quickly to join a companion,
Disappearing into the bakery.
                              Reader, we will never
Know anything about these people or what
Sorrows they carry, tucked away in their
Pockets like a cell phone or a tissue.

Poem Written to Win a Contest

A poem written to win a contest should have
A certain insouciance that tonight I can't muster.
This means I should probably give up before
I begin, before I mention all the embarrassing things
Happening in the lives of people who don't
Read *New England Review* or *Poetry Northwest*.
What life isn't pathetic if you look closely enough,
Open the refrigerator door to find the jar of pesto
That's not green anymore? When did you buy it,
And what did you expect when, instead of spooning it
Thickly onto tuna steaks and searing them in an iron
Skillet till the parmesan melted and browned, you
Ordered-in a pizza with beige canned mushrooms and what
They said were onions? Now, that jar of pesto has gone black
With disappointment, but the only Americans who even
Know what pesto is are the ones who watch the
Food Network and take notes. The really embarrassing
Stuff happens in the neighborhoods that can't keep
A Burger King out of bankruptcy, where the malls
Are boarded up and only the church parking lots are full,
Where guys with more time than money urinate
Behind the schoolyard hedge, and the off-brand gas station
Covers its overhead selling six-packs and tallboys
That disappear into brown paper bags. They're
The alcohol equivalent of a comb-over; it doesn't fool
Anybody, but it's a kind of courtesy that doesn't cost extra.
Elsewhere, sitting around a secondhand kitchen table,
First-round editorial assistants are bent over their laptops,
Pulling contest submissions up from Submittable.
They've read too many poems about someone's
Skin that someone else loved touching. It's made them
Doubt that love exists, or if it does, that anyone
Should write about it, at least not for contests.
Their job is to distinguish the awful and the boring from

The poems their editor might at least want to glance at.
Not another sestina or, worse yet, a villanelle. And,
God knows, not poems about people who work at
Jobs that don't pay enough for a subscription to
The Food Network or HBO or who start their day
With a six-pack. A good contest entry should
Juxtapose maple syrup and melted butter balanced
On a short stack so it doesn't dribble off
With a traffic accident where somehow no one
Was killed. The narrator unbuckles his seat belt,
Brushes pellets of glass off his Levis, takes one of
Those I'm-so-happy-to-be-alive breaths, and decides
To go back to his wife who has been unfaithful—
Or maybe the poem doesn't tell you he does that, but
You sort of know he will because he remembers
Those pancakes, and it's an objective
Correlative for his life, except that nobody uses
Terms like that anymore—and the speaker already
Takes himself way too seriously to slip past those
First readers to reach their editor, who is also
Stuck at a laptop reading submissions, much less
To reach the final judge, who will read ten entries
Sifted out from at least four hundred. The judge,
Who is reasonably famous, will open an email
Attachment, read the poems with a thoughtful
Expression, choose the most insouciant, and return
To a short stack of pancakes with maple syrup and butter.
This poem will not be among the winners.

PREPARATIONS

Bags of the good red onions are hard to find
When shelves are empty before a hurricane.
The bread's run out, and only meat is left,
Defrosting quickly now the power's off.

When shelves are empty before a hurricane,
You take whatever others left behind.
Defrosting quickly now the power's off,
A naked chicken drips into a pan.

You take whatever others left behind—
This is what comes from having ignored the signs.
A naked chicken drips into a pan.
You're lucky to have charcoal and a grill.

This is what comes from having ignored the signs,
The shifting path, the warning to put up shutters.
You're lucky to have charcoal and a grill.
Outside, the winds begin to shake the trees.

The shifting path, the warning to put up shutters,
Reports from planes that flew into the eye—
Outside, the winds begin to shake the trees,
And coconuts fly loose across the lawn.

Reports from planes that flew into the eye
Confirm the course, the thickness of the wall,
While coconuts fly loose across the lawn.
Hurricanes wobble as they near dry land.

Confirm the course, the thickness of the wall,
And pull a mattress up above your head.
Hurricanes wobble as they near dry land,
But not enough to turn back out to sea.

You squeeze your extra batteries in the dark,
Say, "*something, something,* onions were hard to find."
No one can hear you over the sound of wind.
"The bread ran out, only meat was left."

BLACK OLIVES

When I first moved here, I regretted
The loss of my garden, my fruit trees,
Loquats, mangos, longans and lychees,
Avocados and a Brazilian
Tree whose name I forget. The yard was
Barely big enough to hold them all.
Here, the side yard is shaded by huge
Black olive trees. There is little light, and
Despite their name, black olives do not
Give fruit. There's no room for planting trees
Of any kind. In the afternoons
Though, I look out the sliding-glass doors
And see thin trunks of umbrella trees
Forcing their way up through the paving
Stones of the patio. Invasive,
And destructive, they remind me how
Easily this small yard next to the
Sand trap and ninth hole of a golf course
Could go back to the kind of swamp they
Call a hammock, how the monstera
Vines could squeeze tendrils under the roof
And the house return to rotting wood
And dirt. The opossums and raccoons
Would start prowling in daylight. You and
I would have to move elsewhere, maybe
A small apartment downtown, and I'd
Remember that bench by the back fence
And regret losing those black olives.

On a Blue Tarp

The hive was behind the fascia, just below the roof on the west side of the house. Bees kept finding their way inside, flying toward the kitchen lights or the sliding-glass door behind the living room. For months, I tried to help them get out, thirty or more a day. I listened for their buzzing, bumping against the glass and would move quickly with an envelope to scoop them up and outside when I opened the door. The concept of glass was beyond them, but the bees could see sun and foliage. Later, I realized this wasn't going to stop anytime soon, and I started calling around. If the hive had been attached to a tree or under the overhang of the roof, they could have been moved somewhere else, sent to a bee farm, somewhere with acres of crops to pollinate. The man who came out cut a rectangle in the fascia, then poisoned them and brought the honeycomb out in pieces. He showed it to me, all broken up on a blue tarp. I have a picture on my phone.

Stewed Fruit

Not long after I broke up with Wendy and was learning the rules of divorce, the transfer of kids for Wednesday night dinner or for weekend stays, the court hearings where her lawyer proclaimed this the worst case of hidden assets he'd seen in 20 years and I realized he was talking about me—not long after that, I would cook stewed fruit for Toby and Hadley when they'd stay over. Star Market, which was just down the street, had a bin with big plastic bags full of bruised or overripe fruit: yellow and black bananas, oranges no one wanted, mealy pears, and apples with birthmarks, maybe from bouncing across the linoleum floor. For 50 cents or a dollar, you could get 5 lbs or more of these, delicious when cooked quickly over high heat, the bananas first, at the bottom, to make the liquid to cook the rest. The easy way would have been to turn the heat to low and cover them, but that way they curdle. It's better to stand there and stir, blowing on the wooden spoon to taste how sweet they become. In all the depositions, interviews, mediations, and testimony, I don't think anyone ever asked about the stewed fruit I made those mornings for breakfast.

Pastoral of the Alligator Farm

When the full-grown gator leapt in the air,
His jaws snapping closed on a frozen rat,

The audience all inhaled together. The icy
Carcass had been real, dripping rat-water
In the Everglades heat, and the alligator

Had looked asleep until he jumped—or
She jumped. No one checked its

Reproductive organs, just the long jawbone,
The teeth, and the improbable flight
Straight up without wings and the crash

Of brown water when he came back down.
Later, the airboat ride and the captured

Burmese python in a glass cage, the ducks
Waddling on the edges of a pond, demanding
Pellets you bought at a white booth with

Peeling paint. Later, the involuntary glance
At a motionless alligator behind the fence.

FROM A DISTANCE

The sun has already dropped low and
The light turned gold. The brown and blue of
Earth in late November turn as well,
The dense green of black olive trees and
Philodendron mixing with sky, dirt,
And the air that has no color. I
Said yesterday that I loved this light,
How it slips through the bushes, tinting
The cars in the parking lot, the black
Asphalt street, sidewalks, and windowpanes
Of the high-rise apartments to the
East of where we were standing. Later,
We walked along the canal and stared
At headlights crossing the horizon
Like shooting stars. It sounds idyllic,
But only if you're careful where you
Look. On the next street, there's a house where
Two people were murdered last week. I
Passed by the television truck and
The police cars when I walked the dog,
Saw yellow crime-scene tape stretched across
The driveway. It was a two-story
With a fountain in front. The owner's
Son told the press it was a rental
And there was a lot of blood. Now, the
Tape is gone, and someone has cleaned up
The mess. If there aren't any details,
It's because they only matter to
Someone else—family, or someone
Who knew them as more than a story
On a news show. I didn't. I kept
Walking, by the same canal where we
Walked later, looking at the crescent
Moon and constellations. When the dog
Stopped to bury his nose in the grass,
I stared at a blue helicopter

Hovering over the house, taking
Videos of the swimming pool, the
Empty patio, and tired police
Investigators moving back and
Forth across the landscaped yard. That night,
The lights of police cars and broadcast
Trucks were pools of yellow, purple, and
Red on the wet surface of the street.
From a distance, it looked beautiful.

A Story on the Radio

I heard a story on the radio about
A woman killed in Kansas City, a shot
Fired through her window from the street, no mention
Who had shot at what. I looked at my hands
On the steering wheel, remembered Shreveport
In '63 or '64, my father
Driving one evening to the airport to pick up
Partners from St. Louis who were coming
For an inspection. He was going to take them out
For dinner, but on the way, someone fired
A bullet through the window of the station wagon.
It passed from the driver's side to the passenger's,
Somehow, and didn't hit anyone. Just broke
Glass and made four men get drunk that night.
It only takes an inch or two to change our
Lives, billiard balls ricocheting off green felt.
Some slide into the pockets, others don't.
Whoever fired from those streets and houses north
Of Hollywood Avenue disappeared before
The police ever heard what happened. Whoever fired
Couldn't have known who was in the car, what
They looked like, or where they were from. I'll call
Him "the shooter," just as anonymous as
The persons he tried to hit, or not. The rifle was
Probably a .22 because the hole was small.
It might have been just a kid shooting in the dark,
At the lights or at the moon. I had a .22 also,
Stored in my father's closet, but I never
Killed anything—my efforts at hunting
Embarrassing at best. My father came home
Shaken, breath smelling of bourbon—
He didn't want to discuss it.

READING ORWELL IN COLOMBIA

While you tended your father in the nursing home, I sat
In the shade, nodded occasionally to residents and nurses,
And watched the white geese splashing in a pond.

We were south of Cali, a suburb with green fields nearby,
Estates behind white walls, cattle grazing, riders exercising horses.
On the side of the highway, there were families who'd crossed

The mountains from Venezuela and were headed south, children
With small backpacks, blue and pink, as though they'd gone
For a day hike, one that might last the rest of their lives—

Some were asleep. Others, grown men, begged for pesos or
Sold bottled water or energy drinks. I could feel it itching
At the back of my brain, but the thought never made it into words.

This couldn't last forever. My whole life, I've been lucky.
I've never had to leave my country and start over, without
My grandfather's books, the family paintings, Chinese vases.

You ask me if your apartment is "chaotic." I laugh and say no,
And every time I'm there, I think how you assembled it all from
Almost nothing, how much each book, each photo, matters.

You say, joking, when you got here you missed the strikes. "They
Happened all the time." Now, there are barricades across
The highway between Cali and Pance—not something wooden

Out of *Les Misérables*, but the serious kind built by people
Who've had practice, beams of corrugated metal, braced, connected,
Something designed by engineers. I read Homage to Catalonia, but

I didn't pay attention. I missed it. Everything has consequences,
An insurrection in Washington or a general strike in Colombia—
Someone on YouTube says that the *policía* wait until dark, then fire

At every shadow, and a friend writes from Pereira that
Paramilitaries threaten the lives of doctors who treat protestors.
His life has been threatened also. There's nothing

We can do but send text messages, emails. We say,
"Stay safe. Be careful." But it doesn't mean much.
The world is not as well-built as those barricades in Cali.

Governments are made of glass and string, rubber bands and
Lots of paper. In Cali, the police station reminded me of
A huge block of concrete, a relic of civil war, guards with

Automatic weapons—but it's a façade. Your sister in Pance
Writes she only has food to last the week. In Barcelona,
The leftist parties did Franco's work for him, shooting

Each other, declaring everyone else collaborators and criminals.
Orwell escaped to France and back to England. The republic fell.
From here in Miami, I read that a new wave of protests

Is starting soon in Cali, that the humanitarian corridor has
Been closed. We don't know who is safe and who isn't.
Two years ago, I was reading Orwell in Colombia.

—May 11, 2021

SUCKER PUNCH

Can we just admit that it feels good
To outlive someone who did you harm?
My friend Richard called tonight to say

Benny S. died. There'd been a picture
Of him in the paper. Fifty years
Ago, he'd punched me on the side of

The head at a demonstration. My
Glasses flew off, and I went down on
The grass, dazed. For the record, it was

A sucker punch, but the result would
Have been the same regardless. My friends,
Mike Walker and a woman whose name

I'm embarrassed I don't recall, helped
Me up and got me out of there just
As the police charged down from the hill

Where they'd been waiting. They needed a
Fight to break out so they could say we
Were rioting and make some arrests.

Soon after that, I left Shreveport to
Go up north to college. Later, I
Heard Benny had been a boxer and

Done the police a favor. I heard
As well that he was a Klansman. If
That were true I wouldn't be surprised.

The police and the Klan were pretty tight
Back then and maybe still are. Who knows?
I remember, though, that the park was

Shady with oaks and pine trees, dense green
Lawns, and picnic tables. There was an
Old swing set a few feet away, and

Behind us, the parking lot where we
Escaped. I don't recall who drove, just
That I gave someone my keys, maybe

The woman who'd helped me up and said,
"We gotta go." I could see the white
Helmets of police, rushing into

The crowd as we left. I was lucky,
Nothing broken, and I hadn't blacked
Out. The commissioner who'd ordered

The attack died disgraced. He's best known
For having ridden a horse into
A black church, a true son of a bitch,

And Richard says that Benny's obit
Listed lots of grandchildren but no
Wives—not sure what that means. It doesn't

Seem likely he had much of a life.
A better person than I am might have
Stayed in Shreveport, done more, changed more.

Instead, I left because I could leave.
I'm not proud of it, but that's the truth.
What I wanted wasn't there, and what

Was there didn't look like it would change
Real soon. I've only been back twice since
My parents died. But, I miss friends who

Stayed, and I'm sorry I've forgotten
The name of the woman who helped me
Get up and handed back my glasses.

In the Absence of Coffee

In their city, poets were given no special consideration. They leased
Apartments on the upper floors of readers' thoughts, a few rooms,
Comfortable but not showy: the table and chairs inherited
From a previous resident, a bed, a television, and some books.

Informed that barbarians gathered at the border, their response
Was initially skeptical, having read Cavafy. But they also remembered
His poem about Phernazis the Cappadocian and kept working,
Typing on their laptops or, if there was no electricity, scratching notes

On any kind of paper. Soon, like everyone else, they hid in basements,
Learned to distinguish the sounds different types of missiles make
When approaching a target, maybe the housing complex
Next to the supermarket or the park with its statue of a surly

Eminence they used to joke about, the one they took selfies in front of.
How serious he looks, how disapproving.
Is the statue still there? Or does it only exist on a hard drive
Or in a notebook or memorized so that it can't be lost unless

Its poets are lost? When pet dogs wander off, they head for the forest
Where they turn feral, kill rabbits and squirrels, scavenge for carrion
In the snowbanks. But poets don't have the luxury of going feral.
In the ruins of a shopping mall, they make fires out of dictionaries,

Warm their hands over encyclopedias. When there are no more
Slices of cake or milky tea, no more tables in cafés, or waiters
Who recognize them, who inquire how the book is coming along,
They make do with a swallow of something wet and compose

Irregular sonnets while filling sandbags to hold off Caesar's legions.
In the absence of coffee, they write about mixing the dark grounds into
Soil for the garden and pinwheels spinning to keep away sparrows and crows.
In the absence of gardens, they write about coffee, how the machine

Hissed with steam and they'd close their eyes for the first sip.

IX.

From where I'm sitting, I can hear you whisper.

For All the Relatives I Never Knew

This poem is for the great-uncles and the cousins,
For the ones who lived in Kentucky, whom I never met,
For the ones in New Orleans, who lived in the Garden District—
Their son was a bridge champion, now and then mentioned in the papers—
For the ones in Arkansas, who probably knew my father,
For the ones in Mobile, who may or may not exist,
For the ones in New Mexico we lost track of after my great-aunt died,
For the ones in Missouri and Ohio, in Colorado, and even those
Who never left Europe. There are still cousins in France,
Though I couldn't explain the relationship or remember their names.
My mother used to keep track of these things, but she didn't
Write them down. They were in her head, a kind of map of who was
    where and why they were important or why
She had decided not to care about them anymore. On my father's side,
There were people who made family trees, and a few on my mother's.
These ended up in boxes stuffed into closets, something
That no one threw away but no one really wanted to keep.
By now, I've lost touch with just about everybody. Some of them
Died, and some just lived their lives walking in a different direction
From where I was headed. My first cousin in Little Rock was like that,
And she had a sister in Atlanta. Another first cousin lives
In Mexico. She's an artist and has a house on a lake in Jalisco.
I'm not sure, but we might have lived in New York at the same time
And never known it. My father had three brothers, and I barely knew
    any of them.
The one in Toledo, my father's twin, I met a few times.
That was always odd. He looked like my father but didn't sound like
    him.
He stayed up late at night listening to talk radio from all over the
    country and ran a box factory that his wife inherited.
He had two children. One, I was friendly with for a while,
But the other, his daughter, never seemed to like me much.
Now, they've disappeared into marriages and divorces, children, moves,
    new homes, old homes,

Faces in photographs I wouldn't recognize.
Strange to think that nothing links us to each other, except the word
    "family," which doesn't mean anything really.
When I was teaching in Boston, a colleague at the same college turned out
    to be my third cousin.
We discovered it one night talking about families.
An ancestor, August Picard, who fled France after killing an officer in a
    duel, had written his autobiography.
My undiscovered cousin had read it as well and quickly called his uncle,
    also undiscovered, to confirm how we were related.
We got together once or twice for coffee after that, but I'm bad at keeping
    up with people.
I close my eyes for a second and think about the relatives I used to know
    and all the relatives I never knew,
About the velocity of our lives, moving away from each other in the dark
And our curiosity that there may be someone like us,
Sharing a scrap of history, memories of a few faces, a few funerals
Where we paid our respects, the occasional wedding.

Cold Tea

The mint tea has grown cold waiting for
Me to drink it. Already, it's late.
You were writing or translating at
The dining room table. I was here
By the window looking at my face
Reflected in the dark. The dog hears
Something I don't and wants to go out
To investigate. I pretend not
To notice. It's been a long week. I
Don't trust what I read in the papers,
And I'm tired of not being able
To see friends and drink coffee in a
Noisy café. Will there be any
Cafes left by next spring or summer?
The dog has settled down. Whatever
Was moving outside is quiet now.
We can see winter constellations
Again. The Pleiades rise above
The treetops and the shopping mall. Clouds
Move off to the west. I can hear you
Taking a shower, putting on your
Nightgown. You've probably already
Plugged in your cellphone and turned back the
Sheets. In Berlin or Paris, people
Are doing the opposite, getting
Up, putting on their clothes, going to
Work or wanting to, checking their
Pockets for mask, cellphone, and car keys,
Their stars all vanished in gray autumn
Light, their lives just as disrupted as
Ours. I turn off the desk lamp and lean
Back in my chair. In the moonlight, I
Spot an opossum on the back fence.
The tea is cold, but it still tastes good.

—October 5, 2020

PANELA

We shave panela
From a brown lump
Once the size and
Shape of a baseball.
The kitchen knife
With the black handle
Scrapes along a
Precipice, a cliff's
Edge, tough, slippery.
The coffee is
Waiting. You have to
Work for sweetness.

Biscayne Bay

On Biscayne Bay, the high-rise apartment buildings
Shoulder up against each other for a better view of the ocean.
The sun has that intensity it gets in March. I can feel the heat

Through my jeans, the radiation of a star touching my thigh,
My knee. At lunch, we change tables three times to find some
Shade while we wait for our first restaurant meal in over a year,

Unsure where to put our masks, wondering if the vaccines
Will still protect us if we move inside. The food, though, isn't
Worth the anxiety or the sun: processed chicken sandwiches,

French fries extracted from a bag in someone's freezer. It's
The kind of meal to make you appreciate your own cooking,
But walking home, we stop at a bakery to buy a skinny

Loaf of sourdough Italian bread for dinner, watching while
The baker works dough to shape Tuscan rounds. It makes
Me feel better to see it—remembering nights when the streets were

Utterly silent and even the parking lots were empty. Somehow,
The world is coming back to itself. Seagulls fly east toward the bay,
Slipping between the apartment buildings. An Italian baker

Slides round planets of dough into a waiting oven.

—March 22, 2021

146

There's Always a River

In these cities I've loved, there's always
Been a river, a canal, or pier
Rising on stilts above a harbor,
Small boats knocking against some pilings.
At low tide, there'd be shells, rotting wood,
Glimmers of rusted metal—and soon,
A few night fishermen casting their
Lines into the black air and water.
When I was eighteen, I walked along
The Seine from Île Saint-Louis down to
Montparnasse. Later, the Zattere
In Venice, the North End in Boston,
And Biscayne Bay here in Miami—
I don't have souvenirs of any
Of those nights, just the sound of traffic,
Footsteps on cobblestones or pavement,
A wind that smelled damp, sometimes fishy,
Lights reflected on the streets, voices
Of locals and tourists chattering
In French or Italian, Portuguese,
Or something Slavic. I never took
Photographs, and when no one's around
To remember, they'll cease to exist.

ASTRONOMY

The sun already set, the evening star
Sinks, no longer evening, no longer star.

I didn't see it dive, sputtering below
The trees, invisible but still a star.

In the morning, sleeping, I'll miss that brief flash
Smothered by light, another invisible star.

Tonight, when it's late, we'll pass by darkened houses,
Gas stations, stores, just streetlamps and a star.

A plane swings south toward the ocean, its light
Reflected in a sluggish canal, a star.

Walking together through the park at night,
We follow a firefly moving like a star.

Writing About Your Country

In the next room, you are writing about your country,
About a man who wouldn't leave his farm and was killed
By paramilitaries, about hillsides thick with trees,
Green moss covering a stone, a boulder. It makes me
Think of our friend Federico, who practices medicine
In a small town in the Andes. I hunted for it on the map,
And it was hard to find. The pictures on Google showed
A white church and narrow streets, nearby mountains,
Clouds that seemed close. In the next room,
You are close also, closer than clouds hovering
Above a valley or the sound of motorcycles fading
Into something that's almost silence. I can hear a piano,
Passages of Chopin, a disc you're playing on an old
Laptop as you work, a few dates and almonds in a bowl
Within reach, as close as the asylum narratives you
Translated, refugees who applied for visas during
The bad years, years that haven't stopped, *applicants*
Threatened by gangs, by paramilitaries, guerillas—so many
Stories you had to find words for in cold, precise English,
Voices you transposed from Colombia or Venezuela,
Reminding you of relatives in Cali or when you
Taught workshops in Buenaventura, voices to cut
Through the dull gaze of immigration officials,
Their eagerness to finish work, to go play golf or tennis
On the weekend. In the next room, I can hear you
Whispering lines of a poem, the same way I do,
The same way we all do when we write, listening
To ourselves, to our own voices, trying to decipher
The words that will break through our own dull gaze.
In the next room, you are writing about your country,
Which is both far away and close to you. From where
I'm sitting, I can hear you whisper.

PALM FRONDS

You say palm fronds at night remind you
Of Colombia, of the house where
You grew up by the Rio Cali,

The shaded sidewalk between that street
And river, the school next door, the zoo
Around the corner, the steep hill and

Steps leading to your dinner, the noise
Of cars with bad exhausts, evening and
Someone's old record player, notes of

Salsa heard from down the block. You say
There's something "ineffable" at night.
We could be walking in Seville or

Barcelona, to a reading at
Juan Pablo Roa's bookstore or out
For dinner to a restaurant on

La Rambla. There're so many places
We've never seen, towns in Umbria
Or Provence, a harbor with sun-bleached

Houses in the Aegean. Why are
We hungry for these places, talking
About them as we walk—hands touching—

Along a suburban canal in
Miami, powerlines stretching black
Across the moonlight above our heads?

Did the moon shine like this in Cali
Years ago, as you walked thinking of
Madrid, of Paris, the Alhambra?

We'll get there, *mi amor*, I promise.

NOTES

Page 24: After fleeing the Spanish Civil War, Juan Ramón Jiménez and his wife, Zenobia Camprubí, lived in Coral Gables, Florida from 1939 to 1943.

Page 36: On September 26, 1940, in Portbou, Spain, Walter Benjamin was part of a group of refugees ordered by the Franco government to be returned to France. Benjamin, who had previously managed to elude the gestapo, committed suicide.

Page 37: This house, which still stands in Puebla, was built by a powerful man, a converso who had left Spain and prospered in Mexico. He felt so secure in his position that he tiled his house with Stars of David in a challenge to the Inquisition, whose offices were across the street. Finally, power shifted as it always does, and he and his family were imprisoned, probably burned, and the house confiscated. The "Bishop's library" is the beautiful *Biblioteca Palafoxiana*, the oldest public library in the hemisphere.

Page 38: The Song Dynasty poet Su Shi took the name "Su Tung-Po," after the "Eastern Slope," where he was living in exile. Octavio Paz had been Mexico's ambassador to India from 1962 through 1968, when he resigned in protest at the Tlatelolco massacre of students by the Mexican government.

Page 39: Modern renovations to the cathedral at Cuernavaca revealed 17th century frescoes of the capture and martyrdom of Franciscan missionaries in Japan, including the Mexican Felipe de Jesús.

Page 51: From the epigram about the Lacadaemonians (Spartans) who fought at Thermopylae, attributed rightly or wrongly to Simonides of Ceos: "Stranger, go tell the Lacadaemonians that we lie here, obedient to their commands."

Page 60: Wallace Stevens is reported to have lunched once a week at the Hartford Canoe Club, where he would drink martinis.

Page 71: *Apollo and Marsyas*, a 1637 painting by José de Ribera. In the myth, Marsyas challenged Apollo to a musical competition with the winner able to treat the loser however he wished. Apollo won and and chose to flay Marsyas alive for his arrogance.

Page 80: The translation of the last line of the Iliad that is the title of this poem was, I thought, from Lattimore, but it doesn't match my copy of his translation. Perhaps it has shifted in my head over the years, and I creatively misremember.

Page 88: This poem is spoken by Terah, the father of Abraham. Genesis tells us nothing about Abraham's life before he made the covenant and left Ur, but there is a midrash that does. Terah made, sold, and worshipped idols, and Abraham caused a great deal of trouble by smashing them when his father was away and then ironically blaming it on the largest idol.

Page 94: The Beat poet and former advertising copywriter Lew Welch left a suicide note at Gary Snyder's house in the California mountains on May 23, 1971. His body was never found. Kafka died of tuberculosis on June 3, 1924, at a sanitorium just outside Vienna.

Page 100: "Watermelon Man" is a cut from Herbie Hancock's 1962 album, *Takin' Off*.

Page 145: Panela is hard, unrefined whole sugar, usually purchased in the form of a thick block, disc, or ball. It is especially popular in Colombia.

George Franklin practices law in Miami and is the author of *Noise of the World* (Sheila-Na-Gig Editions), *Traveling for No Good Reason* (winner of the Sheila-Na-Gig Editions competition in 2018), the dual-language collection, *Among the Ruins / Entre las ruinas* (Katakana Editores), and a chapbook, *Travels of the Angel of Sorrow* (Blue Cedar Press). He is the co-translator, along with the author, of Ximena *Gómez's Último día / Last Day* and co-author with Gómez of *Conversaciones sobre agua / Conversations About Water* (Katakana Editores).